Apples
Daily Spelling Drills
For Secondary Students

By Susan Kemmerer

Schoolhouse Publishing
659 Schoolhouse Road
Telford, Pennsylvania, 18969
(215)721-9293
www.shpublishing.com

Published by
Schoolhouse Publishing
659 Schoolhouse Road
Telford, PA 18969
(215) 721-9293
www.shpublishing.com

The Scripture quoted in Apples were taken from either the King James Version, the New King James Version, or the New International Version.

The photo of the apple used on the cover is being used by permission, courtesy of the New York Apple Association © New York Apple Association.

Waiver of Responsibility

Using **Apples** is not a guarantee that the user will become a great speller. It is important to use **Apples** in conjunction with individual course work. I encourage the user to read, read, read. Using **Apples** in conjunction with lots of reading *will help* to cement spelling rules in the mind of the user.

© 2005 by Susan Kemmerer

All rights reserved. No part of this publication may be reproduced, stored in a retrieval system, or transmitted in any form or by any means without prior permission of Schoolhouse Publishing, except for individual copies for use within a family by immediate family members.

Dedication

To my third son, Christopher...who was volunteered ☺ to be the guinea pig for this book. Not only did he faithfully do the work, he found my mistakes and corrected them, gave suggestions...and improved his spelling!

Chris, you've been a joy and a delight to teach. I love you! God's hand is so evident in you.

...and to Jesus Christ, my Lord and Savior, who always enables me to apply creativity (even when I felt I had no creativity left) to our homeschool in each situation uniquely for each precious child He has entrusted to me.

Note to parents: I used three different versions of the Bible in creating Apples (KJV, NKJV, and NIV). Generally I chose the version that used words illustrating the spelling rule being studied. Most of the fill-in-the-Bible-verse drills have obvious answers. If the answer isn't obvious, feel free to check the answer key in the back of this book.

Introduction

Do you have a student who can't remember how to spell the most simple words? You go over the spellings of the same words again and again, but within a day he's repeating the same mistakes! His spelling tests are a disaster, and his spelling lists just keep getting longer and longer until they threaten to overwhelm! You know he's not stupid...but when it comes to spelling...well, let's just say he's challenged. If you could take him back through elementary phonics, you would – but he would be insulted by the childish work.

Enter....Apples Daily Spelling Drills for Secondary Students!

Apples simply presents approximately one spelling rule each week, encompassing many of the most important spelling rules. Apples does not dwell on the many exceptions to the rules (although there are notes provided in the back of the book explaining the exceptions). You see, if your student is a poor speller, spelling exceptions are just more confusing!

In Apples, spelling exceptions are presented in separate drills rather than as exceptions to the rules. This will help eliminate confusion and will help the student to concentrate on the many words that do follow the rules, while at the same time teaching them the odd spellings separately.

Apples will help your student to become a more proficient speller by helping him through simple, short, daily drills to memorize the rules. No lists, no tests. Your student simply completes one Apple each day. Every tenth day is a review of previously-learned rules. And the answer key is conveniently provided in the back of the book.

If you have a poor speller, he will probably always struggle in this area – but Apples will keep phonics rules fresh in his mind and give him some of the tools he'll need to improve.

And last, but by no means least, Apples helps the student to apply the rules by completing Scripture, puzzles, and sentences, encouraging him in his faith as well in his academics.

Remember: an Apple a day will help to keep your spelling woes at bay!

Helps

Exceptions: As you know, every spelling rule has exceptions. To a poor speller, exceptions just make spelling even more confusing! For this reason Apples does not present spelling exceptions as part of the drills. Rather, Apples shows the student the many words that do follow the rules. If your student is doing well with the rules, you may choose to have him read the exceptions to the rules in the notes in the back of this book. (The exceptions to each rule are presented separately along with the appropriate lesson numbers for easy reference.) If, however, he is still struggling with a rule, you may choose to forego presenting the exceptions until he is more comfortable with the rule.

Bible versions: In creating drills for Apples, we used three Bible versions: King James Version, New King James Version, and New International Version. We picked the version which used the words/rules being studied. We realize that not everyone has all three versions. As Apples is not intended as a Bible study, we suggest that you don't bog your student down with looking up references in three versions. Here are our suggestions:

- Tell your student that most of the answers will be obvious (each drill contains a word box or list to draw from).
- Those answers that aren't obvious can usually be figured out through the process of elimination.
- Those few that are left can easily be looked up in the answer key. This is actually encouraged, as copying words is an excellent spelling exercise.

Remember: Apples is intended to be quick and easy to use (no more than ten minutes each day). By keeping it simple, Apples minimizes stress in spelling, which enhances learning.

Table of Contents

Adding suffixes	Days 1-5
Beginning syllable "uh" spelled with an -a	Days 6-9
Review	Day 10
Days of the week, months of the year	Days 11-15
Your, you're	Days 16-19
Review	Day 20
When, went, were, and where	Days 21-24
Ending -ch sound spelled as -tch	Days 25-29
Review	Day 30
To, too, and two	Days 31-34
Contractions	Days 35-39
Review	Day 40
Changing -y to -i, adding suffixes	Days 41-49
Review	Day 50
Ending syllable spelled -le	Days 51-54
-I before -e except after -c	Days 55-59
Review	Day 60
Ending syllable spelled -tion	Days 61-65
Was, want, and what	Days 66-69
Review	Day 70
Long -i + t spelled -ight	Days 71-74
Because, before, always, and almost	Days 75-79
Review	Day 80
-Ar sound	Days 81-84
Ending syllable spelled -ture	Days 85-89
Review	Day 90
Any, many, already, and sure	Days 91-94
Ending -j sound spelled -dge	Days 95-99
Review	Day 100
-Or sound	Day 101-104
Do, of, only, and who	Days 105-109
Review	Day 110
Long -a	Days 111-119
Review	Day 120
Long -o	Days 121-129
Review	Day 130
Said, are, and again	Days 131-135
Does, from, have, and can	Days 136-139
Review	Day 140
Long -e	Days 141-149
Review	Day 150
Notes and exceptions	Page 151
Answer key	Page 153

Day 1

Clue: If you are adding a suffix (ending) to a word that
- Ends with a single consonant **AND**
- Has a short vowel sound

Then you double the final consonant before adding the suffix. Some common suffixes that are added are **-ed, -ing,** and **-en.** Don't forget to double the final consonant of a short vowel word before adding these suffixes!

Add the given suffixes to the following words:

Verb	-ed	-ing
slip	slipped	slipping
pat		
clap		
skip		
hop		

Use the words from the chart above to complete the sentences below:
1. Missy was _____ on the ice because she had never skated before.
2. Trevor and Sam _____ more snow between the blocks of the snow fort.
3. The youths _____ their mittened hands to keep them warm.
4. They were _____ up and down to warm their feet.
5. They _____ the big snow battle when it began to rain.

Add the suffix **-ing** to each of the words below by writing out the entire word. Some of the words will not have their endings doubled. Remember the clue!

pin	sing	eat
hang	clip	slap
part	ship	shop
snap	keep	trim

Day 2

> **Clue:** If you are adding a _____ to a word that
> ❖ Ends with a single _____ **AND**
> ❖ Has a _____ vowel sound,
> then you _____ the final consonant before adding the suffix.

1. Add the given suffixes to the following words:

Verb	-ed	-ing
grab		
mop		
bud		
wed		

2. In the story below are a number of short-vowel-with-a-suffix words that have been misspelled. Draw a line through any misspelled words and write the correct spelling on the lines below:

   > In the parable of the Prodigal Son, the youngest son demanded his inheritance immediately. His father sadly sliped the money into a leather bag, and handed it to his son. The young man claped his hands, and grabed the money. Hoping onto the back of a donkey, he slaped its rump and took off. It wasn't long before he spent all his inheritance. It sliped through his fingers like water. He had to go beging for food, and finally took a job sloping pigs. Finally he realized he had been very foolish. Humbly he returned home and beged his father to forgive him. His father huged him and kissed him and welcomed him home.

   _____ _____ _____
   _____ _____ _____
   _____ _____ _____
                _____

Day 3

Clue: If you are adding a _____ to a word that
  ❖ Ends with a single _____ AND
  ❖ Has a _____ vowel sound,
  then you _____ the final consonant before adding the suffix.

1. Add the given suffixes to the following words:

Verb	-ed	-ing
club		
rub		
pit		
trim		
slam		

2. The following words do **not** have the endings doubled when adding a suffix. In the blanks next to each word write an A to indicate reason A, or write a B to indicate reason B.

   A. This word does not have a short vowel sound.
   B. This word does not end in a single consonant.

   ___ jumped   ___ healed   ___ singing
   ___ creeping   ___ praised   ___ helping
   ___ sleeping   ___ panted   ___ testing
   ___ snowing   ___ rained   ___ spoiled

Day 4

> **Clue:** If you are adding a _____ to a word that
> ❖ Ends with a single _____ AND
> ❖ Has a _____ vowel sound,
> then you _____ the final consonant before adding the suffix.

1. The same rule applies to many words with more than one syllable **if** the *final syllable* has a short vowel sound **and** ends with a single consonant. Add the suffix **-ing** to the following words:

   compel_____   upset_____
   forget_____   baby-sit_____
   kidnap_____   expel_____
   combat_____   abut_____
   abet_____   commit_____
   hobnob_____   humbug_____

2. Rewrite the following words, adding the *appropriate* **-ed** ending.

   ram_____   pad_____   camp_____
   lick_____   dip_____   mock_____
   pot_____   lump_____   skin_____
   push_____   chip_____   chop_____
   chill_____   chat_____   bob_____

Day 5

Clue: If you are adding a _____ to a word that
- Ends with a single _____ **AND**
- Has a _____ vowel sound,

then you _____ the final consonant before adding the suffix.

There are 2 misspelled words in each sentence. Circle them and write them correctly on the lines below.
1. When Jesus entered Jerusalem, the people were claping their hands and wavving palm branches.
2. Eleanor was diging up the flowers and poting them in fresh flower pots.
3. We choped some firewood to take campping with us.
4. We should be forgeting what is behind and strivving for what is ahead.
5. Chris skined his knees and elbows and chiped his tooth when he fell off the dirt bike.

___ _____   ___ _____
___ _____   ___ _____
___ _____   ___ _____
___ _____   ___ _____
___ _____   ___ _____

On the short line in front of each of the *above* ten words, write the letter of the reason why the word was wrong. The reasons are listed below.
- A. This word has a short vowel and ends in a single consonant, so the final consonant should be doubled.
- B. This word ends with two consonants, so it shouldn't be doubled.
- C. This word has a long vowel sound, so it shouldn't be doubled.

Add the given suffixes to the following words:

Verb	-ed	-ing
chug		
ship		
dab		
hum		

Day 6

> **Clue:** If a word begins with a syllable that sounds like the "uh" sound, that syllable is usually *spelled with the letter "a"* (as in "abound").

Rewrite each of the words below with the correct spelling.

"uh"bout _____ "uh"gain _____
"uh"lone _____ "uh"round _____
"uh"llow _____ "uh"loud _____
"uh"nother _____ "uh"long _____
"uh"loof _____ "uh"maze _____

Use the words above in the sentences below. One word is used twice.
1. If you love Jesus, don't hold yourself _____ from others.
2. We should love one _____.
3. It is important to witness to others _____ Jesus.
4. The Gospel message must be told _____ the world.
5. Jesus _____ can change our lives.
6. If only we could shout it _____ from the rooftop!
7. _____ Him to change your life.
8. When we follow Jesus, others will follow _____, too.
9. He will defeat Satan _____ and _____.
10. It will _____ others when they see God's power in you.

Circle the misspelled word in each sentence below, and write it correctly on the lines below.

11. Tell me ubout the book you read. Should I read unother one?
12. That was umazing! Did you see how it flew uround?
13. Walk ulong the river. It is peaceful to walk ulone.
14. Will you ullow me to take a turn? I'd like to try ugain.

_____ _____
_____ _____
_____ _____
_____ _____

Day 7

Clue: If a word begins with a syllable that sounds like _____, that syllable is usually spelled with the letter _____.

Rewrite each of the words below with the correct spelling.

"uh"bandon _____	"uh"bility _____
"uh"gain _____	"uh"bove _____
"uh"bout _____	"uh"bound _____
"uh"bide _____	"uh"bolish _____
"uh"buse _____	"uh"cross _____

Use the words above in the sentences below.
1. Should we continue in sin that grace may _____?
2. Christians have suffered much _____ in the past.
3. Paul sailed _____ the Mediterranean Sea.
4. If the ship were to sink, you would have to _____ it.
5. I didn't hear you. Could you say that _____?
6. Abraham Lincoln worked hard to _____ slavery.
7. The Gospel of John is a book _____ the life of Jesus.
8. Set your eyes on things _____, not on things of the Earth.
9. Jesus said that we should _____ in Him.
10. Cindy has the _____ to play many hymns by memory.

Each of the words below starts with the "uh" sound. Write the word correctly and state the letter of the spelling rule.

Reasons:
   A. The first syllable sounds like "uh" *alone*, so it's spelled "a."
   B. The first syllable sounds like "uh" *combined with a consonant*, so it is spelled with a "u".

"um"brella _____ ___		"uh"bout _____ ___
"uh"gain _____ ___		"up"setting _____ ___
"uh"round _____ ___		"ug"ly _____ ___
"um"pire _____ ___		"uh"maze _____ ___

Day 8

> **Clue:** If a word begins with a syllable that sounds like _____, that syllable is usually spelled with the letter _____.

Use the following words, spelling them correctly in the sentences below.

"uh"way	"uh"larm	"uh"dapt	"Uh"laska
"uh"dopted	"uh"fraid	"uh"gainst	"uh"gree
"uh"live	"uh"muse	"uh"head	"uh"mount
"uh"part	"uh"pology	"uh"roma	"uh"shore

1. The ship's captain yelled, "All _____!"
2. The election polls showed George W. Bush _____ of Gore.
3. To paraphrase, we should only be _____ of fear itself.
4. "Behold the Lamb of God who takes _____ the sin of the world." John 1:29
5. Use a precipitation gauge to measure the _____ of rainfall.
6. "No weapon formed _____ thee shall prosper."
7. Brittany set the _____ for 7:00 in the morning.
8. It's much easier to take a puzzle _____ than to put it together!
9. When we _____ together in prayer, God answers!
10. Missionaries must learn to _____ to a new culture.
11. Please make a sincere _____ to your brother.
12. Jesus is _____!
13. The largest state is _____.
14. Josh was hired to _____ the children at the party.
15. Yum! Smell that _____!
16. We have been _____ as children into God's family.

Day 9

Clue: If a word begins with a syllable that sounds like _____, that syllable is usually spelled with the letter _____.

Each of the words below starts with the "uh" sound. Write the word correctly and state the letter of the spelling rule.

Reasons:
A. The first syllable sounds like "uh" *alone*, so it's spelled "a."
B. The first syllable sounds like "uh" *combined with a consonant*, so it is spelled with a "u".

"uh"stonish _____ ___   "un"derneath _____ ___
"uh"tomic _____ ___   "uh"while _____ ___
"un"cle _____ ___   "uh"ware _____ ___
"up"roar _____ ___   "uh"stray _____ ___
"uh"wake _____ ___   "uh"ward _____ ___

Circle each misspelled word in the sentences below, and write it correctly on the lines below.

1. It's ubout time to start the day. Make sure he is uwake.
2. Don't be ufraid. Jesus is ulive!
3. Were you uware of that? I was ustonished, too.
4. It is nice, once in uwhile, to get uway to pray.
5. Please accept my upology. I promise I won't do it ugain.
6. I would like to move to Ulaska, but it would be difficult to udapt.
7. Even though I went ustray, He was willing to udopt me as His child.

_____   _____
_____   _____
_____   _____
_____   _____
_____   _____
_____   _____
_____   _____

Day 10 – Review

> **Clue:** If you are adding a _____ to a word that
> ❖ Ends with a single _____ **AND**
> ❖ Has a _____ vowel sound,
> then you _____ the final consonant before adding the suffix.

> **Clue:** If a word begins with a syllable that sounds like_____,
> that syllable is usually spelled with the letter _____.

Fill in the blanks with the correct words and spellings: "Uh"laska, uh-gainst, bid+ing, uh-way, uh-gain, beg+ing, spit+ing, uh-nother, win+ing, bat+ing

1. The northern-most state, it's capital is Juneau. _____

2. Another way to say, "please leave" is "please go _____."

3. If you are in first place, you are said to be _____.

4. Camels and llamas are known for doing this when angry. _____

5. When you are calling out prices you'd like to pay for items during an auction, you are said to be _____.

6. "Jesus is returning" is the same as "Jesus is coming _____."

7. The number given to a baseball player which shows how often he hits the ball compared to how many times he is at bat is called his _____ average.

8. The Bible tells us that we should love one _____.

9. The Bible asks, "If God be for us, who can be _____ us?"

10. Psalm 37:25 "….I have not seen the righteous forsaken nor his seed _____ bread."

Day 11

> **Clue:** The days of the week are spelled as follows:
>   Sunday, Monday, Tuesday, Wednesday, Thursday, Friday, Saturday.
> All seven end with the word "day."
> The months of the year are spelled as follows:
>   January, February, March, April, May, June, July, August, September, October, November, December.   The last four end with the syllable "ber."
> Always capitalize the first letter of the names of days and months.

1. Though it sounds like a short u, the first vowel in *Monday* is actually an _____.

2. Though it sounds like the oo sound, the first two vowels in *Tuesday* are actually _____.

3. The second vowel in *Wednesday* is silent. It is the letter _____.

4. The er sound in both *Thursday* and *Saturday* is spelled with the letters _____.

5. What letter in *February* is often not pronounced? _____

6. The le sound at the end of *April* is spelled with the letters _____.

7. The long i sound in *July* is spelled with the letter _____.

8. The short i sound at the end of *August* is spelled with the letter ____.

9. The s sound in *December* is spelled with the letter _____.

10. The three-letter word at the end of each name of the days of the week is _____.

11. What same three letters are at the end of the first two months? ____

12. The aw sound in *August* is spelled with what two vowels? _____

13. The days and months all begin with what kind of letter? _____

Day 12

> **Clue:** The days of the week are spelled as follows: _____, _____, _____, _____, _____, _____, _____
> All seven end with the word "_____."
> The months of the year are spelled as follows: _____, _____, _____, _____, _____, _____, _____, _____, _____, _____, _____, _____
> The last four end with the syllable "_____."
> Always _____ the first letter of the names of days and months.

Fill in the blanks with the correct words. Don't forget to capitalize them!

1. Most people go to church on _____.

2. Many churches have midweek services on _____.

3. In the United States, Independence Day is celebrated on the 4th of _____.

4. Christmas is celebrated in the month of _____.

5. Easter is celebrated in the month of _____ or _____, but is always on this day of the week: _____.

6. We celebrate Thanksgiving in the month of _____, and it is always celebrated on this day of the week: _____.

7. Valentines Day is celebrated in the month of _____.

8. Most school children have the weekends off from school. Which two days make up the weekend? _____ and _____.

9. Congress passed a law so that many holidays, regardless of the day on which they actually fell, would be celebrated on _____.

10. For many school children, the school year begins in _____ or _____.

11. The day after Monday is _____.

Day 13

Clue: The days of the week are spelled as follows: _____, _____, _____, _____, _____, _____, _____
All seven end with the word "_____."
The months of the year are spelled as follows: _____, _____, _____, _____, _____, _____, _____, _____, _____, _____, _____, _____
The last four end with the syllable "_____."
Always _____ the first letter of the names of days and months.

1. The Jewish Sabbath is celebrated on what day of the week? _____

2. Mother's Day is in the month of _____.

3. Father's Day is in the month of _____.

4. Though many Christians don't celebrate it, Halloween is in the month of _____.

5. For many people, payday is on _____.

6. The day before Wednesday is _____.

7. The first month of the year is _____.

8. What day is the middle of the typical work week? _____.

9. Election Day is always held on what day of the week? _____.

10. The day before Friday is _____.

11. The second month of the year is _____.

12. The last month of the year is _____.

13. The eighth month of the year is _____.

Day 14

> **Clue:** The days of the week are spelled as follows: _____, _____, _____, _____, _____, _____, _____
> All seven end with the word "_____."
> The months of the year are spelled as follows: _____, _____, _____, _____, _____, _____, _____, _____, _____, _____, _____, _____
> The last four end with the syllable "_____."
> Always _____ the first letter of the names of days and months.

The months are numbered 1-12 in order. When writing them out, place a comma between the day and the year. In the exercise below, write out the full dates given. (Ex: 12/25/00 is December 25, 2000)

1. The Declaration of Independence was signed on 7/4/1776.
   _____

2. The first day of the new millenium was 1/1/00.
   _____

3. George Washington's Birthday was 2/22/1732.
   _____

4. When is your birthday? _____

5. The first man landed on the moon on 7/19/69. _____

6. Martin Luther King, Jr., was assassinated on 4/4/68.
   _____

7. Pearl Harbor was attacked on 12/7/41. _____

8. The stock market crashed on "Black Thursday," 10/24/29.
   _____

9. 6/6/44 is also known as "D-Day" -the beginning of the end of WWII.
   _____

10. 8/15/45 is also known as "VJ-Day" - the end of WWII.
    _____

Day 15

> **Clue:** The days of the week are spelled as follows: _____, _____, _____, _____, _____, _____, _____.
> All seven end with the word "_____."
> The months of the year are spelled as follows: _____, _____, _____, _____, _____, _____, _____, _____, _____, _____, _____, _____.
> The last four end with the syllable "_____."
> Always _____ the first letter of the names of days and months.

1. The day before Sunday is _____.

2. The days before and after Wednesday are _____ and _____.

3. Spring and summer begin in the months of _____ and _____.

4. Autumn begins in the month of _____.

5. Winter begins in the month of _____.

6. Leap year is determined by the month of _____.

7. One month that has no American holiday is the 8th month, _____.

8. New Year, Valentines Day, and Easter are celebrated in the months of _____, _____, and _____.

9. Easter, Mother's Day, and Father's Day are celebrated in the months of _____, _____, and _____.

10. Independence Day, Labor Day, and Halloween are in the months of _____, _____, and _____.

11. Thanksgiving and Christmas are celebrated in the months of _____ and _____

Day 16

> **Clue:** How to remember the difference between "you're" and "your."
> - "You're" is the contraction for "you are." The "a" has been removed, and has been replaced with an apostrophe. If you replace the form of "yoor" in the sentence with the words "you are," and it still makes sense, use "you're."
> - "Your" shows possession. The "r" is not separated by an apostrophe because it belongs to the word – hence the possessive.

Use "your" or "you're" in the sentences below. Only two of them will use the contraction "you're." The rest will use the possessive "your." Remember the test: Does "you are" make sense in the sentence?

1. What is _____ name?

2. Don't forget to put _____ shoes away.

3. Ginny, you should send _____ brother a card.

4. Please watch where _____ going.

5. Did you finish _____ school work?

6. _____ baby brother is so sweet!

7. Could I have _____ recipe for chocolate chip cookies?

8. The paint job on _____ dirt bike is great!

9. We would like you to share _____ testimony this Sunday.

10. This week's Bible study will be at _____ house.

11. I hope _____ planning to be there!

12. _____ idea was terrific!

13. Tell _____ father that I said hi.

Day 17

Clue: How to remember the difference between "you're" and "your."
- _____ is the contraction for _____. The "___" has been removed, and has been replaced with an apostrophe. If you replace the form of "yoor" in the sentence with the words "_____," and it still makes sense, use "_____."
- "_____" shows _____. The "___" is not separated by an apostrophe because it belongs to the word – hence the possessive.

Use "your" or "you're" in the sentences below. Only two of them will use the possessive "your." The rest will use the contraction "you're." Remember the test: Does "you are" make sense in the sentence?

1. I hope _____ not planning to go out without a jacket.

2. _____ supposed to give thanks in everything.

3. If _____ going to be home for dinner, you'll have to hurry.

4. _____ an unlikely candidate for that job.

5. Make sure to do _____ job well.

6. _____ bound to be pleased with the results.

7. It's easy to get distracted when _____ praying.

8. _____ pleasing the Father when you walk by faith.

9. Please clean up when _____ done eating.

10. I heard _____ saving up for a car.

11. If _____ careful with money, you'll have that car in no time.

12. _____ life is in God's hands.

Day 18

> **Clue:** How to remember the difference between "you're" and "your."
> - _____ is the contraction for _____. The "___" has been removed, and has been replaced with an apostrophe. If you replace the form of "yoor" in the sentence with the words "_____," and it still makes sense, use "_____."
> - "_____" shows _____. The "___" is not separated by an apostrophe because it belongs to the word – hence the possessive.

Use "your" or "you're" in the sentences below. Remember the test: does "you are" make sense in the sentence?

1. Rejoice! _____ a child of the King!

2. Next, _____ supposed to turn left on Broad Street.

3. Please put _____ guitar away before little Marah breaks it.

4. _____ supposed to hold the door open for a lady.

5. _____ not going to be out late, are you?

6. _____ friend, Justin, called earlier.

7. _____ supposed to call him back as soon as possible.

8. Put _____ tithe in that envelope.

9. When you tithe, _____ honoring God with _____ money.

10. Did you remember to tell _____ mother "I love you" today?

11. _____ dad said _____ a hard worker.

12. _____ now finished with today's assignment.

Day 19

Clue: How to remember the difference between "you're" and "your."
- _____ is the contraction for _____. The "___" has been removed, and has been replaced with an apostrophe. If you replace the form of "yoor" in the sentence with the words "_____," and it still makes sense, use "_____."
- "_____" shows _____. The "___" is not separated by an apostrophe because it belongs to the word – hence the possessive.

Use "your" or "you're" in the sentences below. Remember the test: Does "you are" make sense in the sentence?

1. _____ to love God with all _____ heart, with all _____ soul, with all _____ mind, and with all _____ strength.

2. _____ also supposed to love _____ neighbor as _____ self.

3. I assume _____ relationship with the Lord is as it should be.

4. When it is as it should be, _____ going to find _____ self with _____ mind fixed on Him.

5. _____ heart will sing praises to Him.

6. _____ going to want to tell others about how incredible He is.

7. _____ going to go through some tough trials, too.

8. When _____ going through these trials, God's power can be displayed in _____ life.

9. _____ not going to be disappointed in _____ life in Christ!

Day 20 Review

Clue: The days of the week are spelled as follows: _____, _____, _____, _____, _____, _____, _____
All seven end with the word "_____."
The months of the year are spelled as follows: _____, _____, _____, _____, _____, _____, _____, _____, _____, _____, _____, _____
The last four end with the syllable "_____."

Clue: How to remember the difference between "you're" and "your."
- _____ is the contraction for _____. The "___" has been removed, and has been replaced with an apostrophe. If you replace the form of "yoor" in the sentence with the words "_____," and it still makes sense, use "_____."
- "_____" shows _____. The "___" is not separated by an apostrophe because it belongs to the word – hence the possessive.

Clue: If you are adding a suffix (ending) to a word that
  ❖ Ends with a single _____ **AND**
  ❖ Has a _____ vowel sound,
then you _____ the final consonant before adding the suffix.

1. _____(yoor) birthday is in _____ (month) and _____(yoor) _____(plan+ing) a birthday party.

2. _____(yoor) _____(get+ing) everything _____(yoor) heart desires, right? (Not!)

3. If _____(yoor) expecting to get everything done, _____(yoor) going to have to order the cake by _____(day after Wednesday).

4. Actually, _____ (beg+ing) and whining get you nowhere.

5. _____(shop+ing) will need to be done, too.

Day 21

> Clue: How do you keep the words *when, went, were,* and *where* straight?
> - *When* speaks of time. It has a silent "h" just like the word *hour*.
> - *Went* is the past tense of the verb *go*. There are no silent letters in either of those two words.
> - *Were* is the past tense of the verb *be*. Both *we* and *were* start with the same letters. These words are often used together: *We were* playing.
> - *Where* speaks of place. The word *here* answers the question *"Where?"* Notice, also, that the word *here* appears in the word *where*.

Use the words *when* and *where* in the following sentences.
1. _____ are we leaving?

2. _____ are we going?

3. Do your eyes water _____ you eat that hot salsa?

4. I can't remember _____ I put that book.

5. _____ and _____ is the Bible Study tonight?

6. _____ do you think you can be ready to go?

Use the words *went* and *were* in the following sentences.
1. Judah _____ to the Borden's Bible Study again.

2. _____ you planning on going also?

3. I think they _____ expecting everyone to bring a friend.

4. Then if we _____, it wouldn't be an imposition?

5. Not at all. If you _____, they'd be blessed.

6. Since you _____ planning on going, then I'll go, too.

7. If we _____ with you, _____ you planning on doing the driving?

Day 22

> Clue: How do you keep the words *when, went, were,* and *where* straight?
> - _____speaks of time. It has a silent "___" just like the word *hour*.
> - _____is the past tense of the verb_____. There are ____silent letters in either of those two words.
> - _____is the past tense of the verb _____. Both "____" and "_____" start with the same letters. These words are often used together.
> - _____speaks of place. The word _____answers the question *"Where?"* Notice that the word _____appears in the word_____.

Find the misspelled words in the sentences below. Circle them, then write them correctly in the spaces following the sentences.

1. Wen where you going to write that thank you note?
   _____, _____

2. When I was your age, I always wanted to be wear my mother was.
   _____

3. Magda whent to the prayer and praise meeting after you where done cutting her hair. _____, _____

4. Where they still singing when you whent home? _____,
   _____

5. How where they supposed to know wen to stop? _____,
   _____

6. We where singing praises until very late, but we finally whent home.
   _____, _____

7. That was the kind of meeting were people where sorry to leave.
   _____, _____

8. The Spirit of the Lord moved on our hearts wen we emptied ourselves.
   _____

9. Wen Christians gather, Christ is in the midst of them. _____

Day 23

Clue: How do you keep the words *when, went, were,* and *where* straight?
- _____ speaks of time. It has a silent "___" just like the word *hour*.
- _____ is the past tense of the verb _____. There are _____ silent letters in either of those two words.
- _____ is the past tense of the verb _____. Both "____" and "_____" start with the same letters. These words are often used together.
- _____ speaks of place. The word _____ answers the question *"Where?"* Notice that the word _____ appears in the word _____.

Use the words *when, went, where,* and *were* in the sentences below.
1. I remember _____ I was a little girl, we _____ to Disney World in Florida.

2. At that time we _____ still in elementary school.

3. We _____ excited to go _____ Mickey and Pluto lived!

4. _____ else could you visit all your favorite cartoon characters?

5. I also remember _____ my grandparents visited us.

6. _____ did they come from? Germany!

7. We _____ unable to understand each other _____ we talked.

8. They _____ only able to speak German, and we _____ only able to speak English.

9. My father speaks both English and German, so that's how we _____ able to communicate.

10. We _____ to Niagara Falls with them.

11. They _____ having a great time...and we _____, too!

Day 24

> Clue: How do you keep the words *when, went, were,* and *where* straight?
> - _____ speaks of time. It has a silent "___" just like the word *hour*.
> - _____ is the past tense of the verb _____. There are _____ silent letters in either of those two words.
> - _____ is the past tense of the verb _____. Both "____" and "_____" start with the same letters. These words are often used together.
> - _____ speaks of place. The word _____ answers the question *"Where?"* Notice that the word _____ appears in the word _____.

Find the misspelled words in the sentences below. Circle them, then write them correctly in the spaces following the sentences.

1. Wen the elections of 2000 where held, history was made.
   _____ , _____

2. The two main candidates where Vice President Al Gore and Texas Governor George W. Bush. _____

3. The two candidates wer poles apart on the issues. _____

4. Wen many people whent to the poles, they had no idea whom they would vote for president. _____ , _____

5. Ware wer you at 3:00AM wen Mr. Gore withdrew his concession?
   _____ , _____ , _____

6. For a while it looked as if Gore won the popular vote, while the electoral vote whent to Bush. _____

7. We wer all challenged in our political convictions. _____

8. Did the elections of 2000 show that we wer not in charge of choosing our president – God is? _____

9. The Bible tells us that wen God's people humble themselves and pray, wen they seek God's face and turn from their wicked ways – that is wen God will hear us and heal our land. _____ ,
   _____ , _____

Day 25

> Clue: When a short-vowel word ends with the -*ch* sound, it is usually spelled with a -*tch*. For exceptions to this rule, see the notes in the back of this book.

Using the clues given, write the correct -tch word in the blank.

batch	catch	crutch	ditch
Dutch	fetch	match	patch
pitch	scratch	watch	witch

1. Another word to describe a toss or throw of a ball: _____

2. A small stick with a coated end used to start a fire: _____

3. To receive or grasp of a ball that has been tossed to you: _____

4. An evil person who derives power from Satan, and uses that power to curse people or direct their destinies: _____

5. A prop that you use when you break a leg: _____

6. A small clock that you wear on your wrist: _____

7. One group or recipe of cookies is called a _____ of cookies.

8. Jack and Jill went up the hill to _____ a pail of water.

9. When a cat unsheathes his claws, he may try to _____ you.

10. People from Holland or the Netherlands are known as _____.

11. A long trench used for drainage is known as a _____.

12. If you get a hole in your pants knee, cover it with a _____.

Day 26

> Clue: When a short-vowel word ends with the -ch sound, it is usually spelled with a _____. For exceptions to this rule, see the notes in the back of this book.

Before completing this exercise, please read the exceptions to the rule for lessons 25-29 on page 151 in the back of this book.
Use the words in the box to complete the sentences below.

watch	wretch	pinched
match	botch	finch
hitch	crutch	bunch
catch	which	witch
fetch	bench	much

1. People like sitting on a park _____.

2. You use a _____ to tell time.

3. Dogs like to play "_____ the stick."

4. A gold _____ likes to eat thistle seed.

5. If you break a leg, you may need to walk with a _____.

6. If you aren't careful, you might _____ the job.

7. How _____ snow are we supposed to get tomorrow?

8. You use a _____ start a fire.

9. "Amazing grace, how sweet the sound, that saved a _____ like me."

10. Before going on vacation, _____ the camper to the van.

11. There were eight bananas in that _____.

12. Did you ever get your fingers _____ in a closed door? Ouch!

13. My boys enjoy trying to _____ the fly balls at the baseball stadium.

Use the words "which" and "witch" correctly in the sentence below.
14. _____ _____ is _____.

Day 27

> Clue: When a short-vowel word ends with the -*ch* sound, it is usually spelled with a _____. For exceptions to this rule, see the notes in the back of this book.

Before completing this exercise, please read the exceptions to the rule for lessons 25-29 on page 151 in the back of this book.
Find and circle the misspelled words in the sentences below. Write the words correctly on the lines provided.

1. For luntch we had fresh tomatoes picked from the garden pach out back, and so mutch sweet corn, it almost made me sick. We also made a bach of cookies for dessert.

_____ _____ _____ _____

2. Our chicken eggs were about to hach. We wanted to wach the chicks as they were born. We sent Mich to fech the camera so we could remember the moment forever.

_____ _____ _____ _____

3. My family came to wach me play baseball. Tyler wound up for the pich. It was my job to cach every ball that came over the plate. There was sutch cheering when we finally won the game.

_____ _____ _____ _____

4. We were camping in the Adirondack Mountains. When we went to unhich the camper, I pintched my fingers in the mechanism. Then I burnt my finger with the mach! I hoped I wouldn't boch up any other chores!

_____ _____ _____ _____

Day 28

> Clue: When a short-vowel word ends with the *-ch* sound, it is usually spelled with a _____. For exceptions to this rule, see the notes in the back of this book.

Use the –tch words from the word box to complete the sentences below.

patch	stitch	pitch	stretch
match	hutch	scratch	clutch
crutch	hitch	Dutch	catch

1. If you _____ that rubberband too far, it will break!

2. There's a song called "_____ a Falling Star and Put It in Your Pocket."

3. If you sprain your ankle, you will need to walk with a _____.

4. When shifting gears, you need to step on the _____.

5. If you hurt your eye, you should cover it with a _____.

6. If you cut your head, you may require a _____.

7. If you had poison ivy, you would want to _____ it.

8. If you live in the Netherlands, you would speak _____.

9. In baseball, the pitcher will _____ the ball.

10. You compare two things to see if they _____.

11. In the old days, you would _____ your horse to a cart.

12. If you have pet rabbits, you would keep them in a _____.

Day 29

> Clue: When a short-vowel word ends with the -*ch* sound, it is usually spelled with a _____. For exceptions to this rule, see the notes in the back of this book.

Find and circle the misspelled words in the sentences below. Write the words correctly on the lines provided. *In order to complete this lesson properly, you must study the exception note for this lesson in the back of the book on page 151.*

1. We lit a tortch for Christmas, and placed it on the front portch of the churtch. The flame grew too large and almost caught the birtch tree on fire!

_____ _____ _____ _____

2. I had a huntch my mother was in a pintch when our cousins stopped by unexpectedly! We were just getting ready to eat luntch, so she invited them in to join us. Mom can make any meal strech!

_____ _____ _____ _____

3. Did you ever wach someone who is learning to drive? It's funny how they'll pop the cluch and lurtch forward. It always makes me flintch when I have to ride with a new driver!

_____ _____ _____ _____

4. Once I heard this "cruntch" sound in the cabinet. I figured it was a mouse, so I grabbed the cat, carefully lifted the lach, and threw her in! Well, she didn't want to muntch on mouse! She just wanted me to scrach her back! She's no help at all!

_____ _____ _____ _____

Day 30 Review

Clue: How do you keep the words *when, went, were,* and *where* straight?
- _____ speaks of time. It has a silent "___" just like the word *hour*.
- _____ is the past tense of the verb_____. There are _____ silent letters in either of those two words.
- _____ is the past tense of the verb _____. Both "____" and "_____" start with the same letters. These words are often used together.
- _____ speaks of place. The word _____ answers the question *"Where?"* Notice that the word _____ appears in the word_____.

Clue: When a short-vowel word ends with the *-ch* sound, it is usually spelled with a _____. For exceptions to this rule, see the notes in the back of this book.

Clue: If a word begins with a syllable that sounds like "uh," that syllable is usually spelled with the letter _____.

Referring to the clues above and using the words in parentheses, spell them correctly in the sentences below.

1. I like the lively hymn "I'll fly (uh-way)_____."

2. Remember the carol, "O, Come Let Us (uh-dore) _____ Him"?

3. "(Wen) _____ the Saints Go Marching In" is another song.

4. "Oh, (Ware)_____, Oh, (Ware)_____ Has My Little Dog Gone" has been around since before you (wer)_____ born.

5. Is "(Wach)_____ And Pray" the name of a song?

6. I often find myself humming a (cachy) _____ tune.

7. If you (uh-dore)_____ God as much as I do, you'll sing, too.

Day 31

Clue: How do you keep the words *two, to,* and *too* straight?
- The word *two* is the number 2. You can remember how to spell it because there are <u>t</u>wo <u>w</u>heels <u>o</u>n a bike.
- The word *too* means *extremely* or it means *also.* If you can substitute either of these words in your sentence, use *too.* Notice that there are two o's, which shows an "*extreme*" amount of o's.
- The word *to* is a preposition. Of the three words, this one is most frequently used – so it's a good thing that it's short and sweet☺.

Using the clues from the box, choose the correct form of "to" to complete the sentences below.

1. Can you explain how _____ get these _____ cats _____ stay off the furniture?

2. It's _____ hot _____ play outside today.

3. I wish I had _____ tickets _____ the circus, _____.

4. Are you ever going _____ hang those _____ pictures?

5. I thought that child was _____ young_____ be able _____ play the piano like that!

6. Our family is so big, we need _____ pews when we go _____ church.

7. Those _____ dogs are _____ messy _____ keep in the house.

8. We are going _____ have _____ put the dogs outside.

9. Hey, we're going on vacation _____ Virginia this year, _____!

10. Now is the time for all good men _____ come _____ the aid of their country.

11. How are you ever going _____ learn how _____ spell these words?

12. God will help you _____ learn!

Day 32

> Clue: How do you keep the words *two, to,* and *too* straight?
> - The word _____ is the number ___. You can remember how to spell it because there are **t**_____ **w**_____ **o**_____ a bike.
> - The word _____ means _____ or it means _____. If you can substitute either of these words in your sentence, use *too*. Notice that there are _____ o's, which shows an "*extreme*" amount of o's.
> - The word _____ is a preposition. Of the three words, this one is _____ _____ used – so it's a good thing that it's _____ and sweet☺.

Circle the misspelled word in each Scripture below and write the correct word in the blanks at the end of the sentences.

1. "He delivered me from my strong enemy, from those who hated me, for they were two strong for me." Ps. 18:17 _____

2. "O my soul, you have said too the Lord, 'You are my Lord. My goodness is nothing apart from You.'" Ps. 16:2 _____

3. "Therefore I will give thanks two You, O LORD, among the Gentiles, and sing praises too Your name." Ps. 18:49 _____ _____

4. "The LORD will give strength too His people; the LORD will bless His people with peace." Ps. 29:11 _____

5. "Commit your way two the LORD, trust also in Him, and He shall bring it too pass." Ps. 37:5 _____ _____

6. "Cast your burden on the LORD, and He shall sustain you; He shall never permit the righteous too be moved." Ps. 55:22 _____

7. "You have hedged me behind and before, and laid Your hand upon me. Such knowledge is to wonderful for me." Ps. 139:5,6 _____

8. "For the word of God is living and powerful, and sharper than any too-edged sword, piercing even two the division of soul and spirit, and of joints and marrow, and is a discerner of the thoughts and intents of the heart." Heb. 4:12 _____ _____

Day 33

Clue: How do you keep the words *two*, *to*, and *too* straight?
- The word _____ is the number ___. You can remember how to spell it because there are t_____ w_____ o____ a bike.
- The word _____ means _____ or it means _____. If you can substitute either of these words in your sentence, use *too*. Notice that there are ____ o's, which shows an "*extreme*" amount of o's.
- The word ____ is a preposition. Of the three words, this one is _____ _____ used – so it's a good thing that it's _____ and sweet☺.

Write *to*, *too*, or *two* in the sentences below. Use the clues from the clue box above to help you.

1. Our spiritual armor helps _____ protect us from the enemy.

2. The Bible tells us _____ put on the helmet of salvation.

3. We are supposed _____ put on the breastplate of righteousness, _____.

4. Don't forget _____ gird yourself with truth.

5. We should learn _____ shod our feet, _____, with the preparation of the gospel of peace.

6. There are _____ things that every Christian should carry _____ help him in his walk with the Lord.

7. We are told _____ carry the shield of faith.

8. We are told _____ carry the sword of the Spirit, which is the word of God.

9. The Bible compares the Word _____ a _____-edged sword capable of getting _____ the very center of our being.

10. If a Christian wants _____ be strong, he should learn _____ don the whole armor of God.

Day 34

> Clue: How do you keep the words *two*, *to*, and *too* straight?
> - The word _____ is the number ___. You can remember how to spell it because there are **t**_____ **w**_____ **o**_____ a bike.
> - The word _____ means _____ or it means_____. If you can substitute either of these words in your sentence, use *too*. Notice that there are ____ o's, which shows an "*extreme*" amount of o's.
> - The word ____ is a preposition. Of the three words, this one is _____ _____ used – so it's a good thing that it's _____ and sweet☺.

Circle the misspelled word in each sentence below and write the correct word in the blanks at the end of the sentences.

1. My husband took us too the stock car races this summer. _____

2. I thought I could tolerate to hours of races. _____

3. Little did I know that I would have too sit there for four hours rather than just too hours! _____ _____

4. Surprisingly, I enjoyed it, two! _____

5. About too dozen cars at a time were supposed too race around the track at top speed. _____ _____

6. They weren't supposed two be crashing into each other – but that's what they did – at every turn! _____

7. It was distressing too see cars crashing, and metal and wheels flying; but apparently that is supposed two make it interesting. _____ _____

8. It certainly was interesting too me, to! _____ _____

9. During one particularly bad accident, they had two call the medi-vac helicopter too fly the driver too the hospital. _____ _____ _____

10. I imagine he was thankful he wasn't badly injured, and the race was able too continue. _____

Day 35

> Clue: Contractions are two words put together to form one word. An apostrophe is used to mark the missing letters.
> - In most contractions, the spelling of the first word doesn't change.
> - Instead, two words are squeezed together and letters are left out.
> - An apostrophe is placed where the letters used to be.
> - The trick is to remember how to spell the two words, don't change the spelling, and put an apostrophe where the letters used to be.

List the letters that were replaced by an apostrophe in the following contractions:

Contraction	Missing Letters	Contraction	Missing Letters
doesn't		you'd	
isn't		wouldn't	
I'll		could've	
that's		you're	
they're		would've	
you'll		don't	
you're		they'll	
she'd		we're	

Add the appropriate contractions to the sentences below.

1. I _____ (do not) know where _____ (you are) supposed to put those.

2. I suppose _____ (you will) figure out a spot for it.

3. We _____ (could have) sold it at a yard sale.

4. You _____ (would not) have wanted to do that, though.

5. _____ (they will) probably have sentimental value attached to them.

6. _____ (that is) why _____ (you would) rather keep them.

7. I know _____ (she would) be interested in buying them from you.

Day 36

Clue: Contractions are _____ words put together to form _____ word. An apostrophe is used to mark the _____ letters.
- In most contractions, the spelling of the first word _____ change.
- Instead, two words are _____ together and letters are_____ _____.
- An apostrophe is placed where the letters_____ ___ ____.
- The trick is to remember how to _____the two words, don't _____ the spelling, and put an apostrophe where the letters_____ ____ ___.

What two words make up each of the contractions below?

Contraction	Two Words	Contraction	Two Words
can't		she's	
you're		shouldn't	
hasn't		hadn't	
weren't		could've	
it's		they're	
we're		you'll	
he'll		aren't	

Use the correct contraction in the sentences below.

1. "God _____(did not) send his Son into the world to condemn the world, but to save the world through him." John 3:17

2. "_____(do not) be deceived. God _____ (is not) mocked. Whatever a man sows, that _____ (he will) also reap." Gal. 6:7

3. "If we confess our sins, _____ (he is) faithful and just to forgive us our sins and to cleanse us from all unrighteousness." 1 Jn. 1:9

4. "Put away lying. Speak every man truth with his neighbor, for _____ (we are) members one of another." Eph. 4:25

5. "_____(I am) confident of this very thing, that He which has begun a good work in you will perform it." Phil. 1:6

6. "_____ (I have) hidden your Word in my heart." Ps. 119:11

Day 37

Clue: Contractions are _____ words put together to form _____ word. An apostrophe is used to mark the _____ letters.
- In most contractions, the spelling of the first word _____ change.
- Instead, two words are _____ together and letters are_____ _____.
- An apostrophe is placed where the letters_____ ___ ____.
- The trick is to remember how to _____ the two words, don't _____ the spelling, and put an apostrophe where the letters_____ ____ ___.

Turn the following words into contractions.

Words	Contraction	Words	Contraction
I am		you are	
I will		we have	
who is		you have	
that will		we are	
would not		can not	
is not		who will	
they are		she is	
were not		should have	

Use the correct contractions in the sentences below.

1. Ben _____ (should have) been more careful when he was playing on that old lawn mower.

2. _____ (he will) never forget when the mower flipped over and landed on his leg.

3. He realized he _____ (was not) able to get up.

4. We _____ (were not) sure whether we should call 911 or not.

5. Ben _____(did not) seem to be in pain, but he just _____ (could not) move his leg.

6. The doctor said, "_____(you will) be in the hospital for at least two weeks, then _____ (you are) going to be in a body cast for at least six."

Day 38

Clue: Contractions are _____ words put together to form _____ word. An apostrophe is used to mark the _____ letters.
- In most contractions, the spelling of the first word _____ change.
- Instead, two words are _____ together and letters are _____ _____.
- An apostrophe is placed where the letters _____ ___ ___.
- The trick is to remember how to _____ the two words, don't _____ the spelling, and put an apostrophe where the letters _____ ____ ___.

Turn the words below into contractions. List the letters that were replaced by an apostrophe.

Words	Contractions	Missing Letters	Words	Contractions	Missing Letters
does not			can not		
we have			were not		
they have			we are		
I would			they would		
he is			I am		
we will			who will		
has not			they are		
who is			those will		

Use the correct contractions in the Scriptures below.

1. "_____ (There is) now no condemnation for those who are in Christ Jesus." Rom. 8:1

2. "For _____ (nothing is) impossible with God." Luke 1:37

3. "_____ (I will) praise you, Lord, with all my heart." Ps. 9:1

4. "_____ (It is) written, 'Man shall not live by bread alone, but by every word that proceeds from the mouth of God.'" Matt. 4:4

5. "Delight yourself in the Lord, and _____ (He will) give thee the desires of your heart." Ps. 37:4

6. "Without faith _____ (it is) impossible to please God." Heb. 11:6

7. "_____(we have) all sinned and fallen short of God's glory." Rm. 3:23

Day 39

Clue: Contractions are _____ words put together to form _____ word. An apostrophe is used to mark the _____ letters.
- In most contractions, the spelling of the first word _____ change.
- Instead, two words are _____ together and letters are_____ _____.
- An apostrophe is placed where the letters_____ ___ ___.
- The trick is to remember how to _____ the two words, don't _____ the spelling, and put an apostrophe where the letters_____ ____ ___.

Turn the words below into contractions. List the letters that were replaced by an apostrophe.

Words	Contractions	Missing Letters	Words	Contractions	Missing Letters
are not			have not		
should not			has not		
she is			it is		
who will			they will		
we will			we are		
they are			I would		
we would			you are		

Use the correct contraction in the sentences below.

1. _____ (would not) you enjoy playing in our band?

2. _____ (You are) sure?

3. _____ (We have) got two guitars and a bass.

4. We _____ (are not) professionals, but we enjoy praising God.

5. We also have a drum set, but I think _____ (they are) too loud to enjoy.

6. _____ (Is not) it amazing how quickly you can learn something when you enjoy it?

7. Why _____ (do not) you join us for worship the next time _____ (it is) convenient.

Day 40 Review

Clue: How do you keep the words *two*, *to*, and *too* straight?
- The word _____ is the number ___. You can remember how to spell it because there are **t**_____ **w**_____ **o**____ a bike.
- The word _____ means _____ or it means _____. If you can substitute either of these words in your sentence, use *too*. Notice that there are ____ o's, which shows an "*extreme*" amount of o's.
- The word ____ is a preposition. Of the three words, this one is _____ _____ used – so it's a good thing that it's _____ and sweet☺.

Clue: Contractions are _____ words put together to form _____ word. An apostrophe is used to mark the _____ letters.
- In most contractions, the spelling of the first word _____ change.
- Instead, two words are _____ together and letters are_____ _____.
- An apostrophe is placed where the letters_____ ___ ____.
- The trick is to remember how to _____ the two words, don't _____ the spelling, and put an apostrophe where the letters_____ ____ ___.

Clue: The days of the week are spelled as follows: _____, _____, _____, _____, _____, _____, _____
All seven end with the word "_____."
The months of the year are spelled as follows: _____, _____, _____, _____, _____, _____, _____, _____, _____, _____, _____, _____
The last four end with the syllable "_____."
Always _____ the first letter of the names of days and months.

Use the correct words in the sentences below.
1. We are going _____ ("too") talk about _____ ("too") or three songs.

2. We'll mention some Scriptures, _____ ("too").

3. "_____ (I will) Never Be the Same Again" is an old song.

4. "_____ (Who Is) Like the Lord" is a new song.

5. "_____ (I will) Fly Away" is an old spiritual.

6. "It Was On a _____ ("Toosday") Somebody Touched Me" is a campfire song.

7. Some, though, were touched by God on _____ ("Wendsday").

Day 41

> Clue: When you are adding a suffix (ending) to a word that ends in "y", you should change the "y" to an "i", *then* add the suffix.

In the words below, first complete the rule, then apply the rule to change the given words.

1. To add the suffix *-ed* to a word ending with **"y"**, change the ____ to an ____, and add _____.
   - baby _____
   - marry _____
   - hurry _____
   - worry _____
   - fry _____
   - accompany _____
   - sanctify _____
   - pretty _____
   - carry _____
   - bury _____
   - tarry _____
   - cry _____
   - spy _____
   - occupy _____
   - justify _____
   - dirty _____

2. To add the suffix *-er* to a word ending with **"y"**, change the ____ to an ____, and add _____.
   - merry _____
   - carry _____
   - heavy _____
   - stinky _____
   - lovely _____
   - fluffy _____
   - friendly _____
   - runny _____
   - happy _____
   - sloppy _____
   - pretty _____
   - ugly _____
   - dirty _____
   - stubby _____

3. To add the plural suffix *-es* to a word ending with **"y"**, change the ____ to an ____, and add _____.
   - baby _____
   - spy _____
   - family _____
   - puppy _____
   - penny _____
   - lobby _____
   - company _____
   - enemy _____
   - cry _____
   - lady _____
   - party _____
   - mommy _____
   - hippy _____
   - cabby _____
   - industry _____
   - city _____

Day 42

> Clue: When you are adding a suffix (ending) to a word that ends in "___", you should change the "___" to an "___", *then* add the _____.

In the words below, first complete the rule, then apply the rule to change the given words.

1. To add the suffix *-est* to a word ending with **"y"**, change the _____ to an _____, and add _____.
   - merry_____   runny_____
   - grouchy_____   happy_____
   - heavy_____   sloppy_____
   - stinky_____   pretty_____
   - lovely_____   ugly_____
   - fluffy_____   dirty_____
   - friendly_____   stubby_____
   - funny_____   dizzy_____

2. To add the plural suffix *-es* to a word ending with **"y"**, change the ___ to an _____, and add _____.
   - candy_____   strawberry_____
   - cherry_____   fly_____
   - pony_____   pansy_____
   - belly_____   story_____
   - buggy_____   reply_____
   - pity_____   satisfy_____

Circle the misspelled words in the sentences below, then write the correct spellings on the blanks following each sentence.

3. It was a lovely spring day, and all the ladys were taking their babys for a walk. _____ _____

4. Toddlers accompanyed their mommys as they soaked up the sunshine and admired the wild daisys growing by the road. _____
_____ _____

5. Bunnys hopped through grassy fields shared with sheep and ponys.
_____ _____

Day 43

Clue: When you are adding a suffix (ending) to a word that ends in "___", you should change the "___" to an "___", *then* add the_____.

In the following sentences, circle the misspelled words, and write them correctly on the lines following.

1. Michael was a bit worryed that he wouldn't have enough money saved up to buy a car. _____

2. He was certainly the happyest teenager on the block when one of the ladys from church actually *gave* her car to him!_____
_____

3. The old Camaro was dirtyer and stinkyer than he would have liked, but it was the lovelyest car in the world to him. _____
_____   _____

4. The car needed lots of work, but the expense was justifyed, even though Michael nearly cryed when he received the repair bill.
_____   _____

5. He hurryed to make the necessary repairs, and he babyed that car to the fullest extent his budget would allow. _____ _____

6. He prettyed up the car until it was lovelyer than ever. _____
_____

7. We were the merryest of familys when we waved goodbye to Dale as he accompanyed Michael to the police station to take his driver's exam. _____ _____ _____

8. Michael occupyed the driver's seat when we spyed him pulling into the driveway later that day. _____ _____

9. It's hard to remain satisfyed with his car as pennys melt away to hundreds of dollars worth of repairs. _____ _____

10. He just prays that his engine won't get fryed! _____

Day 44

> Clue: When you are adding a suffix (ending) to a word that ends in a vowel plus "y", do not change the "y" to an "i", or you'll have too many vowels in a row.

In the words below, first complete the rule, then apply the rule to correctly spell the word.

1. To add the suffix *-ed* to a word ending in a **vowel + y**, do not _____ the ____ to an *i*, or you'll have too many _____. Just add the suffix.
   - play _____
   - employ_____
   - spray_____
   - monkey_____
   - honey_____
   - pray_____
   - obey_____
   - fray_____
   - gray_____
   - stray_____
   - money_____
   - toy_____
   - replay_____
   - enjoy_____

2. To add the suffix *-er* to a word ending in a **vowel + y**, do not _____ the ____ to an *i*, or you'll have too many _____. Just add the suffix.
   - play _____
   - gray_____
   - display_____
   - spray_____
   - buy_____
   - repay_____

3. To add the plural suffix *-s* to a word ending in a **vowel + y**, do not _____ the ____ to an *i*. Just add the *-s*.
   - play _____
   - bay_____
   - spray_____
   - monkey_____
   - honey_____
   - pray_____
   - replay_____
   - enjoy_____
   - display_____
   - fray_____
   - gray_____
   - stray_____
   - donkey_____
   - toy_____
   - pay_____
   - obey_____
   - money_____
   - repay_____

Day 45

> Clue: When adding suffixes to words ending with y...
> - When you are adding a suffix (ending) to a word that ends in "___", you should change the "___" to an "___", then add the_____.
> - When adding a suffix (ending) to a word that ends in a vowel + y, do _____ change the _____ to an_____, or you'll have too many _____ in a row.

1. Fill out the following chart, adding the correct ending to each word.

Word	add -s	add -ed	add -er
enjoy			XXXXXXXXXX
spray			
obey			XXXXXXXXXX
play			
employ			
buy		XXXXXXXXXX	

2. Make each of the following words plural by adding -s.

Word	add -s	Word	add -s
joy		boy	
toy		day	
chimney		key	
valley		donkey	
guy		ray	
ploy		trolley	

In the following sentences, circle the misspelled words, and write them correctly on the lines following.

3. The children monkeied around and plaied noisily through the entire seminar, which fraied their mother's nerves._____ _____ _____

4. The mother praied fervently, then spoke with honeied words, "Had you obeied me, I would have enjoied taking you out for ice cream. Instead, though, you toied with the rules, so now we must go home and you must take naps." _____ _____ _____ _____ _____

Day 46

> Clue: When adding suffixes to words ending with y...
> - When you are adding a suffix (ending) to a word that ends in "___", you should change the "___" to an "___", *then* add the_____.
> - When adding a suffix (ending) to a word that ends in a vowel + y, do _____ change the _____ to an_____, or you'll have too many _____ in a row.

In the following sentences certain words have been misspelled, because the author did not follow the spelling rule concerning words that end in a *vowel plus y*. Circle the misspelled words, change the i's back to y's, and write the words correctly on the lines following.

1. A moneied person is rich, buis what he wants, and pais those emploied by him generously. _____ _____ _____ _____

2. The monkeis that were displaied at the zoo enjoied the tois. _____ _____ _____ _____

3. My emploier had graied dramatically this past year due to the many dais when the dropping stock market fraid his nerves. _____ _____ _____ _____

4. In San Francisco the trolleis run over the hills and through the valleis even on holidais. _____ _____ _____

5. Girls and bois enjoied their birthdais while they were young, but generally don't want their ages displaied once they are older. _____ _____ _____ _____

6. Hopefully you have obeied God when He sais that we should have praied without ceasing._____ _____ _____

7. The hardworking guis next door emploied a graier spraier than mine. _____ _____ _____ _____

8. The chimneis graied the skies with smoke as the sun's rais tried to break through. _____ _____ _____

Day 47

> Clue: When you are adding the suffix -ing to a word, do not change the "y" to an "i", or you'll have two i's in a row.

1. Add an –ing to the following words that end with a y. Remember *not* to change the y to an i, or you'll have too many i's in a row.

word	-ing	word	-ing
play		pay	
spray		pray	
obey		fray	
stray		toy	
replay		enjoy	
display		gray	
copy		try	
justify		cry	
hurry		carry	
marry		fly	
accompany		ferry	

2. Fill in the rules for adding suffixes to words ending in the letter y.

   - When a word ends with y, you must change the ____ to an ____ before adding the suffix.
   - When a word ends with a vowel + y, do ____ change the ____ to an ____ before adding the suffix or you will have too many _____ in a row.
   - When adding the suffix –ing to any word ending with a y, do ____ change the ____ to an ____, or you'll have too many ____'s in a row.

3. Using the above rules as reference, circle the misspelled words in the sentence below and write the correct spellings on the following lines.

- God is in the business of justifiing and sanctifiing sinners, and enjois fellowship with us when we are praiing and obeiing Him. _____
  _____ _____ _____ _____

Day 48

Clue: When adding suffixes to words ending with y...
- When you are adding a suffix (ending) to a word that ends in _____, you should change the _____ to an _____, *then* add the_____.
- When adding a suffix (ending) to a word that ends in a vowel + y, do _____ change the _____ to an_____, or you'll have too many _____ in a row.
- When you are adding the suffix -ing to a word, do _____ change the _____ to an_____, or you'll have _____ i's in a_____.

Circle the misspelled words in the sentences below and write them correctly on the following lines.

1. When you spend so much time babiing the little ones in the family, it's always tough when a new baby comes along._____

2. The dethroned child had been enjoiing life as center of the household until the new baby's criing stole all his attention.
   _____ _____

3. Obeiing an inner urge, the older of the two begins displaiing attention-getting devices. _____ _____

4. You'll see him triing to be cute, or he may even try copiing the new baby's mannerisms. _____ _____

5. You might see him triing to act mature, and he may even try carriing his new brother or sister around. _____ _____

6. The older child does not think he's disobeiing – no, but he may be repaiing you for displacing him with another!
   _____ _____

7. Though your nerves may be fraiing and your hair graiing, you will find that toddlers generally LOVE their little siblings very much.
   _____ _____

8. If you spend time praiing for them and plaiing with them, you'll be enjoiing both the toddler and the new baby. _____
   _____ _____

Day 49

> Clue: When adding suffixes to words ending with y...
> - When you are adding a suffix (ending) to a word that ends in _____, you should change the _____ to an _____, *then* add the_____.
> - When adding a suffix (ending) to a word that ends in a vowel + y, do _____ change the _____ to an_____, or you'll have too many _____ in a row.
> - When you are adding the suffix -ing to a word, do _____ change the _____ to an_____, or you'll have _____ i's in a_____.

Fill in the rules for adding suffixes to words ending in the letter y.
  A. When a word ends with y, you must change the ____ to an _____ before adding the suffix.
  B. When a word ends with a vowel + y, do _____ change the _____ to an _____ before adding the suffix or you will have too many _____ in a row.
  C. When adding the suffix –ing to any word ending with a y, do _____ change the _____ to an _____, or you'll have too many ____'s in a row.

Circle the misspelled words in the sentences, then write them correctly on the lines below.
1. Many familys go to church in America, but there are many different churches to choose from.
2. Most Sundaies will see girls and boies going to church, but some churches fill their pews on Saturdaies.
3. At our church the attendees are happyest when they are enjoiing a worship service or fellowshipping with the saints.
4. You'll see worshippers carriing banners and plaiing tambourines, or you'll see saints and sinners praiing and criing before the Lord's altar.

___ _____   ___ _____
___ _____   ___ _____
___ _____   ___ _____
___ _____   ___ _____
___ _____   ___ _____

On the short line in front of each of the above ten words, write the letter of the reason why the word was wrong. The reasons are as A, B, or C at the top of this exercise.

Day 50 - Review

Clue: How do you keep the words *when, went, were,* and *where* straight?
- _____ speaks of time. It has a silent "___" just like the word *hour*.
- _____ is the past tense of the verb _____. There are _____ silent letters in either of those two words.
- _____ is the past tense of the verb _____. Both "____" and "_____" start with the same letters. These words are often used together.
- _____ speaks of place. The word _____ answers the question *"Where?"* Notice that the word _____ appears in the word _____.

Clue: How do you keep the words *two, to,* and *too* straight?
- The word _____ is the number ___. You can remember how to spell it because there are <u>t</u>_____ <u>w</u>_____ <u>o</u>____ a bike.
- The word _____ means _____ or it means _____. If you can substitute either of these words in your sentence, use *too*. Notice that there are ____ o's, which shows an *"extreme"* amount of o's.
- The word ____ is a preposition. Of the three words, this one is _____ _____ used – so it's a good thing that it's _____ and sweet☺.

Clue: When adding suffixes to words ending with y...
- When you are adding a suffix (ending) to a word that ends in _____, you should change the _____ to an _____, *then* add the _____.
- When adding a suffix (ending) to a word that ends in a vowel + y, do _____ change the _____ to an _____, or you'll have too many _____ in a row.
- When you are adding the suffix -ing to a word, do _____ change the _____ to an _____, or you'll have _____ i's in a _____.

Circle the misspelled words in each of the sentences below and write them correctly on the following lines.

1. Wen you're happyer than most people, you know Jesus put that joy in you're heart. _____ _____ _____

2. You need too go were God leads and share you're faith two a lost world. _____ _____ _____ _____

3. Do you remember ware you wer wen President Reagan was shot? _____ _____ _____ _____

4. Wen I whent forward too the altar, you've never seen a sorryer girl. _____ _____ _____ _____

Day 51

> Clue: When a word with two or more syllables ends with the –ull sound, it is usually spelled with an –le.

Rewrite each of the words below by changing the given ending to the correct –le ending.

bottull _____	tabull _____
handull _____	castull _____
steepull _____	waddull _____
dwindull _____	abull _____
paddull _____	cattull _____
bundull _____	chuckull _____

Spelling them correctly, use the words above in the sentences below.
1. The Lord owns the _____ on a thousand hills.
2. Fragile. _____ with care.
3. Ducks _____ clumsily when they walk.
4. During a drought, a stream will _____ to nothing.
5. "Thou preparest a _____ before me in the presence of mine enemies..." Psalm 23:5
6. A baby is a precious _____ of joy.
7. A baby will drink a _____ of milk every few hours.
8. The king and queen live in a _____.
9. A good joke will make me _____.
10. On top of many churches you will see a _____.
11. "I am persuaded that He is _____ to keep that which I've committed unto Him against that day." 2 Tim. 1:12
12. Have you ever been "up a crick without a _____"?

Circle the misspelled words in each sentence below, and write it correctly on the lines below.
1. In a book about a man named Gulliver, Lilliputians were littel peopel.
2. *Jungel Book*, by Rudyard Kipling, is an exampel of a classic.
3. The *Holy Bibel* contains the books of *I and II Chronicels*.

_____   _____   _____
_____   _____   _____

Day 52

> Clue: When a word with two or more syllables _____ with the –ull sound, it is usually spelled with an _____.

Rewrite each of the words below by changing the given ending to the correct –le ending.

1. candull _____ peopull _____
2. littull _____ trampull _____
3. spittull _____ puzzull _____
4. toppull _____ Bibull _____
5. bottull _____ trembull _____
6. cuddull _____ drizzull _____

Circle the misspelled words in the sentences below. Write them correctly on the lines provided.

1. In the story of Noah's ark, it didn't just drizzel – it rained!
2. "He spat on the ground and made clay with the spittel." Jn. 9:6
3. "You have redeemed us to God by Your blood out of every tribe and tongue and peopull and nation." Rev. 5:9
4. "No one, when he has lit a candel, covers it…" Luke 8:16
5. "Desire the pure milk of the word"…but you'll get it in the Bibel, not a bottel. 1 Peter 2:2
6. "Do not… cast your pearls before swine, lest they trampel them under their feet…" Matthew 7:6
7. "Suffer the littel children to come unto Me…" Mark 10:14
8. I can picture Jesus loving to cuddel all those precious children.
9. The Lord told Joshua, "Be strong and courageous. Do not trembel, nor be dismayed, for the Lord your God is with you." Joshua 1:8
10. He knew the walls of Jericho would toppel, even though Joshua might puzzel over God's strange instructions!

_____ _____ _____
_____ _____ _____
_____ _____ _____
_____ _____ _____

Day 53

Clue: When a word with two or more syllables _____ with the -ull sound, it is usually spelled with an _____.

Rewrite each of the words below by changing the given ending to the correct -le ending.

- jingull _____ tempull _____.
- troubull _____ waffulls _____.
- doubull _____ singull _____.
- tangull _____ marbull _____.
- bubbull _____ valuabull _____.
- comfortabull _____ dimpull _____.
- appull _____ scrappull _____.

Use the words above, spelled correctly, in the sentences below.

1. Another word for a church or synagogue is a _____.
2. The Pennsylvania Dutch are famous for a jam-like fruit spread called _____ butter.
3. Another Pennsylvania Dutch treat is to spread the applebutter on slices of pressed meat scraps known as _____.
4. If you are ever treated to a Pennsylvania Dutch breakfast, you might also want to try their pancake-like treats called _____.
5. When something can cause problems in two different areas, it's known as _____ _____.
6. Statues are carved of a beautiful, soft rock called _____.
7. When you shop for new shoes, you want to make sure they are _____ when you try them on.
8. A popular Christmas song is called "_____ Bells."
9. When a person is not married, they are said to be _____.
10. A depression that appears in a person's cheek when he is smiling is known as a _____.
11. When you blow gum, you can form a _____.
12. Another word for a knot is a _____.
13. Because diamonds are rare, they are said to be _____.

Day 54

> Clue: When a word with two or more syllables _____ with the –ull sound, it is usually spelled with an _____.

Rewrite each of the words below with the correct spelling.

- portabull _____ lovabull _____ .
- feebull _____ pimpulls _____ .
- pestull _____ tattull _____ .
- sampull _____ spindull _____ .
- exampull _____ horribull _____ .
- circull _____ rattull _____ .
- cradull _____ terribull _____ .

Use the words above, spelled correctly, in the sentences below.

1. Proverbs 31:19 shows the virtuous woman holding a _____.
2. A baby sleeps in a _____ and, when awake, plays with a _____.
3. These two words both mean "to strike terror or horror into one's heart." _____ and _____
4. Black heads and _____ are called acne.
5. An _____ of an addition problem is 3 + 2 = 5.
6. If you visited Hershey's Chocolate World, you would want to _____ the chocolate.
7. Indians ground corn in a mortar with a _____.
8. A camper is a _____ home.
9. Though they are wild animals, panda bears look _____.
10. The elderly often grow _____ without loving care from their families.
11. Children will sometimes _____ on other children when they want them to get in trouble.
12. A flat, round shape is called a _____.

Day 55

> Clue: Memorize this poem: "i before e except after c, or when it says a as in neighbor and weigh." This means that in words with this vowel combination...
> - If the letter c is first, use an -ei.
> - If the word has the long a sound, use -ei.
> - The above two are uncommon, so mostly you will use an -ie.

In the words below fill in the proper vowel combination. After each word, write an A, B, or C to indicate the rule you used.
   A. Use i before e in most words.
   B. Use ei- if the letter c is in front of it.
   C. Use ei- if the word has the long a sound.

- fr____nd _____
- c____ling _____
- rec____pt _____
- w____gh _____
- n____ghbor _____

bel____ve _____
retr____ve _____
dec____tful _____
f____ld _____
Dan____l _____

th____f _____
____ght(8)_____
p____ce _____
y____ld _____
t____ _____

Circle the misspelled words in the sentences below. Write them correctly on the lines following along with an A, B, or C to indicate the rule you used.

1. We have a Golden Retreiver named Daneil. _____ ___, _____ _____

2. He is ieght years old and wieghs too much to be healthy. _____ ____, _____ _____

3. All our nieghbors see him as a freind. _____ ____, _____ _____

4. Sometimes he acts like a theif and sneaks a peice of meat from the table. _____ ____, _____ _____

5. I beleive he could jump as high as the cieling to retreive a tossed frisbee if he didn't wiegh so much! _____ ____, _____ ____, _____ ____, _____ ____

6. We've never had to tei him up, because he never wanders farther than the feild next door. _____ ____, _____ _____

7. There's not a decietful bone in his loyal body! _____ ___

Day 56

Clue: Memorize this poem: "___ before ___ except after ___, or when it says ___ as in neighbor and weigh." This means that in words with this vowel combination...
- If the letter c is first, use an -_____.
- If the word has the long a sound, use -_____.
- The above two are uncommon, so mostly you will use an -_____.

In the words below fill in the proper vowel combination. After each word, write an A, B, or C to indicate the rule you used.
  A. Use i before e in most words.
  B. Use ei- if the letter c is in front of it.
  C. Use ei- if the word has the long a sound.

- l___ _____   d____ _____   qu___t _____
- th____r _____   conc____ve _____   ch___f _____
- h___r _____   pat____nt _____   fr____nd _____
- y___ld _____   f___ld _____   rec____ve ____
- dec____ved _____   n____ghbor _____   bel___ve ____

In the Bible verses below, use the correctly-spelled words from the above list to fill in the blanks.

1. "Behold, the virgin shall _____ and bear a Son, and shall call His name Immanuel." Isaiah 7:14
2. "...But _____ yourselves to God, and your members as instruments of righteousness to God." Romans 6:13
3. "She considers a _____ and buys it." Proverbs 31:16
4. "...It is impossible for God to _____..." Hebrews 6:18
5. "_____ on the Lord Jesus Christ, and you will be saved, you and your household." Acts 16:31
6. "You shall love the Lord your God...and your _____ as yourself." Luke 10:27
7. "Therefore you are...an _____ of God through Christ." Gal. 4:7
8. "You also be _____. Establish your hearts..." James 5:8
9. "He...said to them, '_____ the Holy Spirit.'" John 20:22
10. "Do not be _____, God is not mocked; for whatever a man sows, that he will also reap." Galatians 6:7
11. "Aspire to lead a _____life, to mind your own business, and to work with your hands..." 1 Thess. 4:11
12. "A _____ loves at all times..." Proverbs 17:17

Day 57

Clue: Memorize this poem: "___ before ___ except after ___, or when it says ___ as in neighbor and weigh." This means that in words with this vowel combination...
- If the letter c is first, use an -_____.
- If the word has the long a sound, use -_____.
- The above two are uncommon, so mostly you will use an -_____.

In the words below fill in the proper vowel combination. After each word, write an A, B, or C to indicate the rule you used.
        A. Use i before e in most words.
        B. Use ei- if the letter c is in front of it.
        C. Use ei- if the word has the long a sound.

- p____ ____
- aud____nce ____
- misch____f ____
- dec____t ____
- qu____t ____

rel____ved ____
conc____t ____
f____nd ____
rec____pt ____
repr____ve ____

th____r ____
v____w ____
rev____w ____
f____rce ____
cash____r ____

Circle the misspelled words in the sentences below. Write them correctly on the lines following along with an A, B, or C to indicate the rule you used.

1. It is important to reveiw before a test. _____ ____
2. An unruly child will cause mischeif. _____ ____
3. The Bible says a meek and queit spirit is beautiful. _____ ____
4. An appreciative audeince will clap loudly. _____ ____
5. Lions and tigers are very feirce. _____ ____
6. Thier house has three bedrooms. _____ ____
7. The casheir will give you a reciept after you make a purchase at the store. _____ ____, _____ ____
8. Eric had to give his speech today, but he was releived when he was granted a repreive. _____ ____, _____ ____
9. Have you ever had shoofly pei? _____ ____
10. The feind was concieted enough to return to the crime scene. _____ ____, _____ ____
11. The veiw from the mountaintop was fabulous! _____ ____

Day 58

> Clue: Memorize this poem: "___ before ___ except after ___, or when it says ___ as in neighbor and weigh." This means that in words with this vowel combination...
> - If the letter c is first, use an -_____.
> - If the word has the long a sound, use -_____.
> - The above two are uncommon, so mostly you will use an -_____.

In the words below fill in the proper vowel combination. After each word, write an A, B, or C to indicate the rule you used.
        A. Use i before e in most words.
        B. Use ei- if the letter c is in front of it.
        C. Use ei- if the word has the long a sound.

- fr____ndly _____
- dec____tful _____
- h____rloom _____
- uny____lded _____
- f____ndish _____

repr____ve _____
pat____ntly _____
rel____ved _____
conc____ted _____
aud____nce _____

th____r _____
qu____tly _____
v____wing _____
th____ves _____
bel____f _____

Circle the misspelled words in the sentences below. Write them correctly on the lines following along with an A, B, or C to indicate the rule you used.

1. The old Bible, printed in 1793, was a valuable family hierloom. _____ ____

2. We were releived when the feindish theives were caught. _____ ____, _____ ____, _____ ____

3. An unyeilded heart is a decietful heart – concieted in its beleif that God is not in control. _____ ____, _____ ____, _____ ____, _____ ____

4. They chose a participant from the veiwing audeince. _____ ____, _____ ____

5. Thier freindly cat sat queitly purring on the visitor's lap. _____ ____, _____ ____, _____ ____

6. Unjustly condemned, the prisoner pateintly awaited a repreive. _____ ____, _____ ____

Day 59

Clue: Memorize this poem: "___ before ___ except after ___, or when it says ___ as in neighbor and weigh." This means that in words with this vowel combination...
- If the letter c is first, use an -_____.
- If the word has the long a sound, use -_____.
- The above two are uncommon, so mostly you will use an -_____.

In the words below fill in the proper vowel combination. After each word, write an A, B, or C to indicate the rule you used.
   A. Use i before e in most words.
   B. Use ei- if the letter c is in front of it.
   C. Use ei- if the word has the long a sound.

- d___t ____   exper____nce ____   ____ghteen ____
- ____ghty ____   br____fcase ____   s____ve ____
- p___rce ____   d____sel ____   n____ce ____
- s____ge ____   n____ghbor ____   th____r ____
- c____ling ____   t____rs ____   unw____ldy ____
- sh____ld ____   p____r ____   p____ty ____

Circle the misspelled words in the sentences below. Write them correctly on the lines following along with an A, B, or C to indicate the rule used.

1. Inside Dad's breifcase you'll find about ieghteen pens.
   _____ _____, _____ _____

2. When Mr. Glumpus went on a deit, he lost ieghty pounds.
   _____ _____, _____ _____

3. Arrows were unable to peirce the Indian's sheild.
   _____ _____, _____ _____

4. My neice didn't have the expereince required for the job.
   _____ _____, _____ _____

5. The men lowered the paralytic right through a hole in thier cieling.
   _____ _____, _____ _____

6. With seven teirs, the wedding cake was too unweildy to move.
   _____ _____, _____ _____

7. During the seige of the city, the monk's peity was a comfort to all.
   _____ _____, _____ _____

8. While the boat was tied up to the peir, we filled it with deisel fuel.
   _____ _____, _____ _____

9. The nieghbor put the applesauce through a seive to get the lumps out.
   _____ _____, _____ _____

Day 60 - Review

> Clue: When a short-vowel word ends with the -*ch* sound, it is usually spelled with a _____. For exceptions to this rule, see the notes in the back of this book.

> Clue: When a word with two or more syllables _____ with the –ull sound, it is usually spelled with an _____.

> Clue: Memorize this poem: "___ before ___ except after ___, or when it says ___ as in neighbor and weigh." This means that in words with this vowel combination...
> - If the letter c is first, use a -_____.
> - If the word has the long a sound, use -_____.
> - The above two are uncommon, so mostly you will use an -_____.

Circle the misspelled words in each sentence and write them correctly on the lines following.

1. We used a small peice of candel wax to temporarily pach the hole.
   _____ _____ _____

2. The nieghbors tried to cach the door handel when it suddenly flew open._____ _____ _____

3. Please fech my neice's bottel out of the diaper bag. _____
   _____ _____

4. Recieve a bach of letters from peopel from other countries through pen pal clubs._____ _____ _____

5. My uncel recieved Jesus as his savior at Sunday's prayer wach service.
   _____ _____ _____

6. How did you handel the news that Jesus was peirced for your sins?
   _____ _____

Day 61

Clue: When a word has a syllable that sounds like "shun," it is *usually* spelled –tion. See the note in the back of the book for exceptions.

Rewrite each of the words below with the correct spelling.

creashun _____	moshun _____
evolushun _____	poshun _____
vacashun _____	capshun _____
noshuns _____	correcshun _____
stashun _____	vaccinashun _____

Use the correctly-spelled words above in the sentences below.

1. You fill up your car with gas at a gas _____.
2. When traveling in a car, some people get _____ sickness.
3. In <u>Snow White</u>, the witch dipped an apple in a magic _____.
4. If you believe in the theory of _____, you believe that life evolved from non-living chemicals.
5. If you believe in _____, you believe that life was specifically designed and brought into being by an intelligent Creator.
6. Descriptive words under a picture are called a _____.
7. Many people will take a _____ to Niagara Falls.
8. For each mistake, you should make a _____.
9. Before visiting a tropical country, you may need a _____ for malaria.
10. Needles, thread, buttons, and scissors are sewing _____.

Circle the misspelled words in each sentence below, and write it correctly on the lines below.

11. The Evolushunist and the Creashunist debated about origins of life.
12. We needed to make a correcshun to the capshun under the picture.
13. We need that vaccinashun before we go on vacashun to Cancun.

_____   _____
_____   _____
_____   _____

Day 62

> **Clue:** When a word has a syllable that sounds like "shun," it is *usually* spelled -_____. See the note in the back of the book for exceptions.

Rewrite each of the words below with the correct spelling.

loshun	commoshun
aucshun	secshuns
ficshun	locashun
acshun	dicshunary
reacshun	menshun

Use the correctly-spelled words above in the sentences below.

1. Always remember to use suntan _____ when you are visiting the beach.
2. Each book of the Bible has been broken into _____ called chapters.
3. Have you ever heard of the song, "Make _____ that His Name is Exalted"?
4. The neighbors sold all their household goods at an _____.
5. If you can't spell it, look it up in a _____.
6. Frank Peretti's The Oath is a work of _____.
7. People usually have a strong _____ to jalapeno peppers.
8. Many little boys play with _____ figures.
9. Put five toddlers in a room, and you will have _____.
10. No one knows the exact _____ of Mount Sinai.

Circle the misspelled words in each sentence below, and write it correctly on the lines below.

11. You'll need to check a dicshunary to check the spelling of *reacshun*.
12. Did I menshun that the aucshun is tomorrow?

_____   _____
_____   _____

Day 63

Clue: When a word has a syllable that sounds like "shun," it is *usually* spelled -_____. See the note in the back of the book for exceptions.

Use the following words, spelled correctly, in the Bible verses below (taken from the King James Version).

tradi"shuns"
sanctifica"shun"
affec"shun"
afflic"shuns"
crea"shun"

condemna"shun"
conversa"shun"
salva"shun"
communica"shun"
prepara"shun"

1. "Let your c_____ be as it becometh the gospel of Christ...) Philippians 1:27
2. "And take the helmet of s_____, and the sword of the Spirit, which is the word of God." Ephesians 6:17
3. "Therefore, brethren, stand fast, and hold the t_____ which ye have been taught..." 2 Thess. 2:15
4. "...Every one of you should know how to possess his vessel in s_____ and honour." 1 Thessalonians 4:4
5. "Many are the a_____ of the righteous: but the LORD delivereth him out of them all." Psalm 34:19
6. "Set your a_____ on things above, not on things on the earth." Colossians 3:2
7. "But now ye also put off all these; anger, wrath, malice, blashphemy, filthy c_____ out of your mouth." Colossians 3:8
8. "The invisible things of him from the c_____ of the world are clearly seen...even his eternal power and Godhead..." Rom. 1:20
9. "There is therefore now no c_____ to them which are in Christ Jesus, who walk not after the flesh..." Romans 8:1
10. "And your feet shod with the p_____ of the gospel of peace..." Ephesians 6:15

Day 64

> **Clue:** When a word has a syllable that sounds like "shun," it is *usually* spelled -_____. See the note in the back of the book for exceptions.

Use the following words, spelled correctly, in the Bible verses below (taken from the King James Version). One word is used twice.

tribula"shun"(s)
supplica"shun"
vexa"shun"
tempta"shun"
visita"shun"

founda"shun"
na"shun"
voca"shun"
transla"shun"
genera"shun"

1. "Praying always with all prayer and s_____ in the Spirit..." Ephesians 6:18
2. "And lead us not into t_____, but deliver us from evil..." Matthew 6:13
3. "By faith Enoch was translated that he should not see death...for before his t_____ he had this testimony, that he pleased God." Hebrews 11:5
4. "And not only so, but we glory in t_____ also: knowing that t_____ worketh patience." (Romans 5:3)
5. "I have seen all the works that are done under the sun; and behold, all is vanity and v_____ of spirit." Ecclesiastes 1:14
6. "They shall not leave in thee one stone upon another; because thou knewest not the time of thy v_____." Luke 19:44
7. "I therefore...beseech you that ye walk worthy of the v_____ wherewith ye are called..." Ephesians 4:1
8. "He is like a man which built an house, and digged deep, and laid the f_____ on a rock..." Luke 6:48
9. "But ye are a chosen g_____, a royal priesthood, a holy n_____, a peculiar people; that ye should shew forth the praises of him who hath called you out of darkness into his marvelous light." 1 Peter 2:9

Day 65

> **Clue:** When a word has a syllable that sounds like "shun," it is *usually* spelled -_____. See the note in the back of the book for exceptions.

Rewrite each of the words below with the correct spelling.

perfecshun _____   consolashun _____
compleshun _____   execushuns _____
damnashun _____   correcshun _____
excepshuns _____   acshun _____
ficshun _____   tracshun _____

Use the corrected words above in the sentences below.

1. Upon _____ of the course, you will receive one credit.
2. The loser of the game received a _____ prize.
3. As the saying goes, truth is stranger than _____.
4. When Ben broke his femur, he was in _____ for three weeks.
5. You should always strive for _____.
6. There are many _____ to this spelling rule.
7. If you misspell a word, the computer makes the _____ for you.
8. In the 1700's it was not uncommon to witness public _____.
9. Those who have not received Jesus as their Lord and savior are in danger of eternal _____.
10. If you haven't accepted Jesus as Lord, I urge you to take _____ right away.

Circle the misspelled words in the sentences below.

11. Though I may never reach perfecshun, I take consolashun in knowing that Jesus loves me just as I am.
12. Upon compleshun of this lesson you won't need spelling correcshun any longer, right?
13. If you are rigged up in tracshun, you will experience no acshun except, perhaps, within the pages of a book.

Day 66

> **Clue:** How do you keep the words *was*, *want*, and *what* straight?
> - *Was* is the past tense of the word *is*. The "uh" sound is spelled with an -a, and there is no -h-. It is a short word, just like all of the "be" verbs.
> - *Want* means *desire*. It does not have an -h, nor an apostrophe. Remember: You *can't* always have what you *want*.
> - *What* is one of the "5 w's" (who, what, where, when, and why). All "5 w's" begin with "wh".

Fill in the blanks with either *was, want, wanted,* or *what*.

1. Who _____ the founder of Pennsylvania?

2. William Penn _____!

3. He _____ to create a colony where love _____ the governing law.

4. He _____ a place where people could worship God as they saw fit.

5. _____ _____ the outcome?

6. He _____ greatly disappointed that the law of love is only strong enough to govern those who will allow themselves to be governed by it.

7. _____ a surprise to find out that most people were more than willing to take advantage of his generosity – to the point of forcing him into debtor's prison!

8. William Penn's holy experiment did not succeed as he had _____ it to, but it did plant seeds of freedom for the successful start of a whole new nation.

9. _____ the framers of the Constitution used as their guidelines for the nation's new government _____ Penn's Pennsylvania Constitution.

Day 67

Clue: How do you keep the words *was, want,* and *what* straight?
- _____ is the past tense of the word *is*. The "uh" sound is spelled with an __, and there is no -__-. It is a short word, just like all of the "be" verbs.
- _____ means *desire*. It does not have an -__, nor an apostrophe. Remember: You _____ always have what you_____.
- _____ is one of the "5 w's" (who, _____, where, when, and why). All "5 w's" begin with "____".

Fill in the puzzle with the words *was, what, wanted,* and *want.*

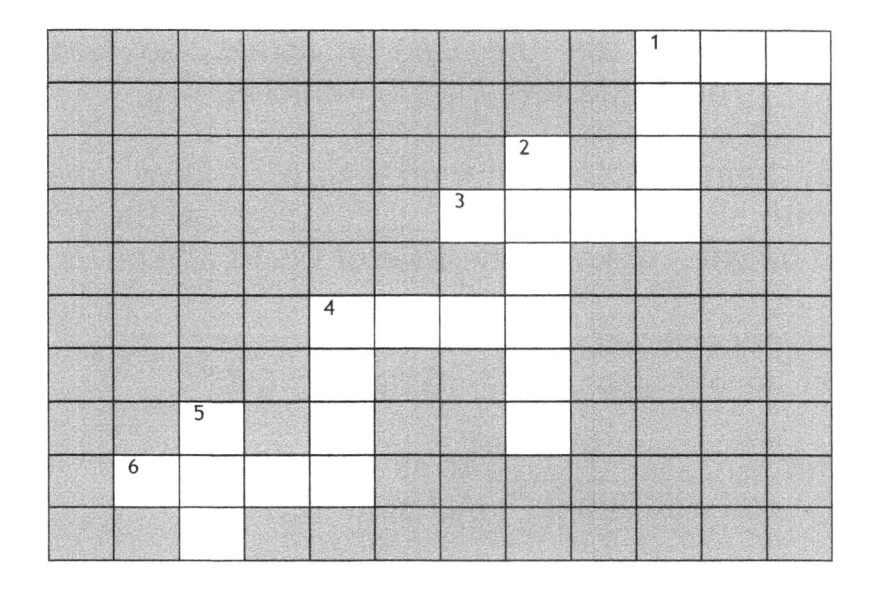

Across

1. "He _____ wounded for our transgressions..."
3. I _____ to be more like Jesus.
4. "_____ a friend we have in Jesus."
6. Do you _____ to spend eternity with Him?

Down

1. _____ has Jesus done in your life?
2. He _____ the whole world to hear the Good News.
4. Do you _____ to get to know Him better?
5. Jesus _____ crucified for our sins.

Day 68

> **Clue:** How do you keep the words *was*, *want*, and *what* straight?
> - _____ is the past tense of the word *is*. The "uh" sound is spelled with an __, and there is no -__-. It is a short word, just like all of the "be" verbs.
> - _____ means *desire*. It does not have an -__, nor an apostrophe. Remember: You _____ always have what you_____.
> - _____ is one of the "5 w's" (who, _____, where, when, and why). All "5 w's" begin with "____".

Use the words *what*, *was*, *want*, and *wants* in the Bible verses below.

1. "And Jabez called on the God of Israel….so God granted him _____ he requested." 1 Chronicles 4:10

2. "That you, being rooted and grounded in love, may be able to comprehend with all the saints _____ is the width and length and depth and height – to know the love of Christ…" Eph. 3: 17-18

3. "Do not be deceived, God is not mocked; for _____ever a man sows, that he will also reap." Galatians 6:7

4. "For whoever _____ to save his life will lose it, but whoever loses his life for me will find it." Matthew 16:25

5. "Now the serpent _____ more crafty than any of the wild animals the Lord God had made…" Genesis 3:1

6. "God saw all that he had made, and it _____ very good. And there _____ evening, and there _____ morning – the sixth day." Genesis 1:31

7. "I know _____ it is to be in need and I know _____ it is to have plenty. I have learned the secret of being content in any and every situation, whether well-fed or hungry, whether living in plenty or in _____. I can do all things through Christ who strengthens me." Philippians 4:12-13

8. "In God, whose Word I praise, in God I trust; I will not be afraid. _____ can mortal man do to me?" Psalm 56:4

Day 69

Clue: How do you keep the words *was*, *want*, and *what* straight?
- _____ is the past tense of the word *is*. The "uh" sound is spelled with an __, and there is no -__-. It is a short word, just like all of the "be" verbs.
- _____ means *desire*. It does not have an -__, nor an apostrophe. Remember: You _____ always have what you_____.
- _____ is one of the "5 w's" (who, _____, where, when, and why). All "5 w's" begin with "____".

Use the words *what, was, want, wanting* or *wanted* in the verses below.

1. "Do not be yoked together with unbelievers. For _____ do righteousness and wickedness have in common? Or _____ fellowship can light have with darkness?" 2 Corinthians 6:14

2. "But let patience have her perfect work, that ye may be perfect and entire, _____ nothing." James 1:4

3. "The Lord is my shepherd, I shall not _____." Psalm 23:1

4. "Pharoah and all his officials and all the Egyptians got up during the night, and there _____ loud wailing in Egypt, for there _____ not a house without someone dead." Exodus 12:30

5. "The young lions do lack, and suffer hunger: but they that seek the LORD shall not _____ any good thing." Psalm 34:10

6. "Saul _____ thirty years old when he became king, and he reigned over Israel forty-two years." 1 Samuel 13:1

7. "Finally, brothers, _____ever is true, _____ever is noble, _____ever is right, _____ever is pure, _____ever is lovely, _____ever is admirable—if anything is excellent or praiseworthy—think about such things. _____ever you have learned or received or heard from me, or seen in me—put it into practice. And the God of peace will be with you." Philippians 4:8-9

8. "And when they _____ wine, the mother of Jesus saith unto him, They have no wine." John 2:3

Day 70 Review

Clue: When a word has a syllable that sounds like "shun," it is *usually* spelled -_____. See the note in the back of the book for exceptions.

Clue: How do you keep the words *was, want,* and *what* straight?
- _____ is the past tense of the word *is*. The "uh" sound is spelled with an __, and there is no -__-. It is a short word, just like all of the "be" verbs.
- _____ means *desire*. It does not have an -__, nor an apostrophe. Remember: You _____ always have what you_____.
- _____ is one of the "5 w's" (who, _____, where, when, and why). All "5 w's" begin with "____".

Clue: How to remember the difference between "you're" and "your."
- _____ is the contraction for _____. The "___" has been removed, and has been replaced with an apostrophe. If you replace the form of "yoor" in the sentence with the words "_____," and it still makes sense, use "_____."
- "_____" shows _____. The "___" is not separated by an apostrophe because it *belongs* to the word – hence the possessive.

Clue: When a word with two or more syllables _____ with the -ull sound, it is usually spelled with an _____.

Circle the correct spelling for the word in each sentence below.

1. (You're, Your) a (tempel, temple) of the Holy Spirit.

2. (Wut, What) kind of (educashun, education) does God (whant, want) you to have?

3. A person's (salvation, salvashun) (whas, was) the most important aspect of (educashun, education) in colonial days.

4. A (simpel, simple) course of study including the 3 R's plus lots of (Bible, Bibel) will equip you to (handle, handel) most of life's (situashuns, situations).

5. (Your, You're) mind also needs the discipline of (addishunal, additional) studies in science and history.

Day 71

Clue: Words that end with a long -i sound plus -t are usually spelled with an -ight. The -gh is silent.

Spell the words correctly in the chart below.

br"ite" _____	f"ite" _____
r"ite" _____	t"ite" _____
l"ite" _____	s"ite" _____

Use the correctly-spelled words above in the sentences below.

1. A _____ smile is one result of having the fruit of joy growing in your life.

2. If you flee temptation as the Bible commands, you will be spared from finding yourself in many _____ spots.

3. "What a _____ that will be when our Jesus we shall see."

4. Jesus is the _____ of the world.

5. "Many sons had Father Abraham. I am one of them, and so are you, so let's just praise the Lord. _____ foot, left foot…"

6. Jesus commands us not to _____, but rather to turn the other cheek and love our enemies.

Circle the misspelled words in the sentences below and write them correctly on the lines.

7. It is not rite for a Christian to fite.
8. The star shown forth with a brite lite.
9. My eye site was blurry because my glasses were too tite.

_____   _____
_____   _____
_____   _____

Day 72

> **Clue:** Words that end with a long –i sound plus –t are usually spelled with an _____. The –_____ is silent.

Spell the words correctly in the chart below.

bl"ite" _____	fl"ite" _____
fr"ite" _____	pl"ite" _____
m"ite" _____	n"ite" _____

Use the correctly-spelled words above in the sentences below.

1. Jonah was really in a _____ when he was swallowed by a great fish.

2. You should love the Lord with all your _____.

3. Jesus will return like a thief in the _____.

4. The "F" he got in English was a real _____ on his school records.

5. Their _____ to JFK International Airport was scheduled to depart at 3:17 PM.

6. You should have seen the look of _____ on his face when we jumped out at him from behind the door!

Circle the misspelled words in the sentences below and write them correctly on the lines.

7. The blite in the corn put the farmer in a real plite.
8. I mite prefer an evening flite if it's less crowded.
9. The child shook in frite when he woke up from a nitemare.

_____   _____
_____   _____
_____   _____

Day 73

Clue: Words that end with a long -i sound plus -t are usually spelled with an _____. The -_____ is silent.

Find 10 "-ight" words in the word search puzzle below. Use the words to fill in the blanks in the sentences below.

1. Cinderella's coach turned into a pumpkin at the stroke of _____.
2. If it isn't wrong, it's _____.
3. Chris replaced the _____ in the lamp.
4. What a _____ God we serve.
5. The sun was too _____ without my sunglasses.
6. What a _____ it was to see a rainbow over the Grand Canyon!
7. Christians _____ the Enemy with the Sword of the Spirit.
8. That parking spot was too _____ to park our big van.
9. I enjoyed the plane _____ over the Grand Canyon.
10. Our souls are _____ by sin.

r	a	w	q	y	o	p	a	s	d	f	g	b
h	i	j	k	l	z	m	x	c	v	b	n	l
m	q	g	w	e	s	i	g	h	t	r	t	u
y	u	i	h	o	p	a	s	d	f	g	h	b
c	x	m	z	t	l	k	j	f	i	g	h	t
v	b	i	i	n	m	q	w	l	e	r	t	h
y	u	g	i	d	o	p	a	i	s	d	f	g
g	h	h	j	k	n	l	z	g	x	c	v	i
b	n	t	m	b	l	i	g	h	t	e	d	l
q	w	y	e	r	r	t	g	t	y	u	i	o
p	a	s	d	i	f	g	h	h	j	k	l	z
x	c	v	b	g	n	m	q	g	t	w	e	r
t	y	u	i	h	o	o	p	i	a	s	d	f
f	g	h	j	t	k	l	z	t	x	c	v	b

bright, blighted, fight, flight, lightbulb, mighty, midnight, right, sight, tight

Day 74

Clue: Words that end with a long -i sound plus -t are usually spelled with an _____. The -_____ is silent.

Complete the puzzle using the clues below.

Across
1. What a _____ God we serve.
2. President _____ D. Eisenhower
5. This burns out and must be changed frequently.
8. We were on _____ 631 from Philadelphia to Atlanta.
9. A word for squeezed or confining.
10. Another word for a plague or disease.

Down
1. Another word for 12:00 AM.
3. When Jesus touched the blind man, he received his _____.
4. Another word for a difficulty or a problem.
6. "_____ shone the moon that night…"
7. The opposite of left.
8. Another word for a bad scare.

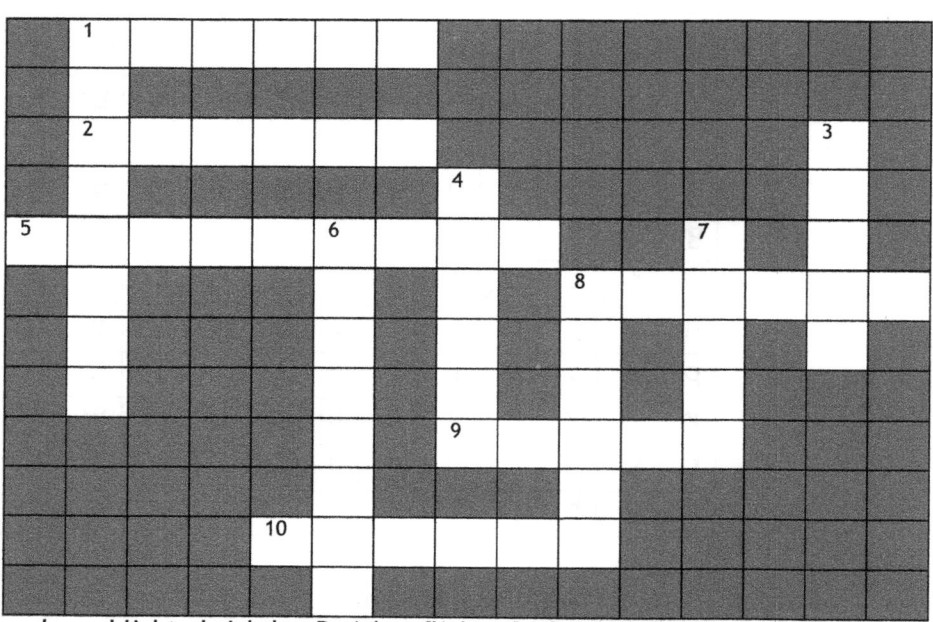

(Answers in alphabetic order: blight, brightly, Dwight, flight, fright, light bulb, midnight, mighty, plight, right, sight, tight.)

Day 75

Clue: The words "because" and "before" both begin with a be- and end with a silent e.
- "Because" has an -aw- sound that is spelled with an -au-.
- "Before" has the word "for" in the middle

The words "always" and "almost" both begin with an al-.
- "Always" ends with the word "ways."
- "Almost" ends with the word "most."

Circle the misspelled words in the sentences below, and write the words correctly on the lines provided. Use *because, before, always,* and *almost*.

1. God allways answers prayer. _____

2. We had to wash the dishes befor we could leave. _____

3. "Becuz He lives, I can face tomorrow." _____

4. It's allmost time to go. _____

Fill in the blanks with either *because, before, always,* or *almost*. Make sure you spell them correctly.

5. _____ look both ways _____ you cross the street.

6. We _____ lost our hay crop _____ it rained so much last summer.

7. We bundled up _____ we went out _____ of the snow storm.

8. We _____ decided not to go to the New Year's parade since it is _____ so cold.

9. We _____ pray when we get together _____ we all love the Lord.

Day 76

Clue: The words "because" and "before" both begin with a _____ and end with a silent _____.
- _____ has an –aw– sound that is spelled with an –_____–.
- _____ has the word "_____" in the middle

The words "always" and "almost" both begin with an _____–.
- _____ ends with the word "_____."
- _____ ends with the word "_____."

Use the words *because, before, always,* and *almost* to complete the Bible passages below.

1. "I will sing unto the LORD _____ he hath dealt bountifully with me." Psalm 13:6

2. "I have set the LORD _____ _____ me: _____ he is at my right hand, I shall not be moved." Ps. 16:8

3. "And all the families of the nations shall worship _____ thee." Psalm 22:27

4. "I was daily His delight, rejoicing_____ _____ Him, Rejoicing in His inhabited world…" Prov. 8:30-31

5. "Watch therefore, and pray _____…" Luke 21:36

6. "And according to the law _____ all things are purified with blood…." Hebrews 9:22

7. "Then God blessed the seventh day and sanctified it, _____ in it He rested from all His work…" Genesis 2:3

8. "Without ceasing I make mention of you _____ in my prayers." Romans 1:9

9. "They _____ made an end of me on earth, but I did not forsake Your precepts." Psalm 119:87

10. "He who answers a matter _____ he hears it, it is folly and shame to him." Proverbs 18:13

Day 77

> **Clue:** The words "because" and "before" both begin with a _____ and end with a silent _____.
> - _____ has an –aw– sound that is spelled with an –_____-.
> - _____ has the word "_____" in the middle
>
> The words "always" and "almost" both begin with an _____-.
> - _____ ends with the word "_____."
> - _____ ends with the word "_____."

Use the words *because, before, always,* and *almost* to complete the Bible passages below.

1. "I love the LORD, _____ he hath heard my voice and my supplications. _____ he hath inclined his ear unto me, therefore will I call upon him as long as I live."   Psalm 116:1-2

2. "Thou preparest a table _____ me in the presence of mine enemies: thou anointest my head with oil…" Psalm 23:5

3. "But as for me, my feet were _____ gone; my steps had well nigh slipped." Psalm 73:2

4. "For our heart shall rejoice in him, _____ we have trusted in his holy name." Psalm 33:21

5. "Then Agrippa said unto Paul, _____ thou persuadest me to be a Christian." Acts 26:28

6. "Take heed that ye despise not one of these little ones;…in heaven their angels do _____ behold the face of my Father." Mt. 18:10

7. "The Father hath not left me alone; for I do _____ those things that please him." John 8:29

8. "Fret not thyself _____ of evildoers, neither be thou envious against the workers of iniquity." Psalm 37:1

9. "For the ways of men are _____ the eyes of the Lord, and he pondereth all his goings." Proverbs 5:21

Day 78

> **Clue:** The words "because" and "before" both begin with a _____ and end with a silent _____.
> - _____ has an –aw- sound that is spelled with an -_____-.
> - _____ has the word "_____" in the middle
>
> The words "always" and "almost" both begin with an _____-.
> - _____ ends with the word "_____."
> - _____ ends with the word "_____."

Use the words *because, before, always,* and *almost* to complete the Bible passages below.

1. "Giving thanks _____ for all things unto God and the Father in the name of our Lord Jesus Christ." Ephesians 5:20

2. "But do thou for me, O God the Lord, for thy name's sake: _____ thy mercy is good, deliver thou me." Psalm 109:21

3. "I was _____ in all evil in the midst of the congregation and assembly." Proverbs 5:14

4. "_____ destruction the heart of man is haughty, and _____ honour is humility." Proverbs 18:12

Circle the misspelled words in the sentences below and write them correctly on the lines provided.

5. "We allways get up very early on Christmas morning becaus we have so many people to visit." _____ _____

6. "Befor man sinned in the garden, he allways fellowshipped with God." _____ _____

7. "The program will allmost be over befor we get there!" _____ _____

8. "He allmost fell out of the tree becauz the squirrel startled him." _____ _____

Day 79

> **Clue:** The words "because" and "before" both begin with a _____ and end with a silent _____.
> - _____ has an -aw- sound that is spelled with an -_____-.
> - _____ has the word "_____" in the middle
>
> The words "always" and "almost" both begin with an _____-.
> - _____ ends with the word "_____."
> - _____ ends with the word "_____."

Use the words *because, before, almost,* or *always* in the sentences below. Make sure you spell them correctly.

1. _____ I knew the Lord, I was _____ very shy.

2. I was afraid of _____ everything.

3. My life was full of fear _____ I had no one to trust in and no one to put my faith in.

4. _____ of my faith in Him, I am no longer afraid and no longer so shy.

5. As it says in Psalm 91:14, "_____he loves me," says the Lord, "I will rescue him. I will protect him _____ he acknowledges my name."

6. Now I am afraid of _____nothing.

7. Where _____ I had fear and insecurity, now _____ of Jesus, I have assurance and comfort.

8. I will _____ praise the Lord for his great mercy in my life.

Day 80 – Review

Clue: Words that end with a long –i sound plus –t are usually spelled with an _____. The –_____ is silent.

Clue: The words "because" and "before" both begin with a _____ and end with a silent _____.
- _____ has an –aw– sound that is spelled with an –_____–.
- _____ has the word "_____" in the middle

The words "always" and "almost" both begin with an _____–.
- _____ ends with the word "_____."
- _____ ends with the word "_____."

Clue: Contractions are _____ words put together to form _____ word. An apostrophe is used to mark the _____ letters.
- In most contractions, the spelling of the first word _____ change.
- Instead, two words are _____ together and letters are_____ _____.
- An apostrophe is placed where the letters_____ ___ ___.
- The trick is to remember how to _____ the two words, don't _____ the spelling, and put an apostrophe where the letters_____ ____ ___.

Clue: When a word has a syllable that sounds like "shun," it is *usually* spelled –_____. See the notes in the back for exceptions.

Using the clues above, circle the misspelled words in the sentences below, then spell them correctly on the lines that follow.

1. We couldint pinpoint the exact locashun where the rocket landed becuz it was not lite enough to see anymore. _____
_____ _____ _____

2. Even though it was rite in front of us, we allmost didint see the train stashun._____ _____ _____ _____

3. More students mite believe in creashun if theyd allways teach evolushun as a theory that is failing._____ _____
_____ _____ _____

Day 81

Clue: When the letters -ar- are blended together, they form the sound that you hear in the word ☆ **star.**

Complete the puzzle below with words containing the "ar" sound.

Across
3. Round shiny object used for playing games. Often lost.
7. Safe place for ships.
9. What you do with your car when you aren't driving it.
10. What you sound in a fire.
11. To reserve. Original.
14. Many people plant one of these.
16. To mend socks.
17. Fourth planet from the sun.
18. A large store.

Down
1. Not near.
2. Not stupid.
4. A wise purchase. Cheap.
5. A vehicle.
6. Cute and precious. Last name of owners of the dog named Lady.
8. Farm animals are kept in here.
9. To excuse.
12. Form of the verb "be."
13. To endanger or hurt.
15. Not light.

(Answers in alphabetical order: alarm, are, bargain, barn, car, charter, dark, darling, darn, far, garden, harbor, harm, marble, market, Mars, pardon, park, smart.)

Day 82

> **Clue:** When the letters -_____- are blended together, they form the sound that you hear in the word ⭐ _____.

Use words from the list below to complete the Scripture passages. One word is used twice.

stars	harm	army	garden
alarm	far	harp	pardon
part	spark s	arm	mark

1. "Blow ye the trumpet in Zion, and sound an _____ in my holy mountain..." Joel 2:1

2. "Hast thou an _____ like God?" Job 40:9

3. "And the Lord shall utter his voice before his _____..." Joel 2:11

4. "O Lord, be not _____ from me." Psalm 35:22

5. "And the LORD God planted a _____ eastward in Eden." Genesis 2:8

6. "And who is he that will _____ you...?" 1 Peter 3:13

7. "Praise him with the psaltery and _____." Psalm 150:3

8. "I press toward the _____ for the prize of the high calling of God in Christ Jesus." Philippians 3:14

9. "For thy name's sake, LORD, _____ mine iniquity; for it is great." Psalm 25:11

10. "For we know in _____, and we prophesy in _____." 1 Cor. 13:9

11. "Man is born unto trouble, as the _____ fly upward." Job 5:7

12. "He made the _____ also." Genesis 1:16

Day 83

Clue: When the letters -_____- are blended together, they form the sound that you hear in the word ☆ _____.

Fill in the blanks in the sentences with the following "ar" words.

1. A container for holding foods like jelly and sauce. _____

2. Gymnasts can do dangerous stunts on the parallel _____.

3. The third month of the year is _____.

4. What Moses did to the water when the Egyptians were chasing the Israelites: _____

5. David, the King of Israel, played an instrument called a _____.

6. A large, dangerous, man-eating fish: _____

7. The school subject where you learn to draw and paint: _____.

8. Old MacDonald had a _____.

9. The opposite of stop: _____.

10. Twinkle, twinkle, little _____.

11. The second gospel: _____.

12. Not stupid. _____

13. A Volkswagen is a type of _____.

14. The tiny flash that starts a fire is called a _____.

15. At the ends of these limbs you have hands: _____.

16. The pointed game piece thrown at a bullseye target: _____.

arms	March
art	Mark
bars	part
car	shark
dart	smart
farm	spark
harp	star
jar	start

Day 84

Clue: When the letters -_____- are blended together, they form the sound that you hear in the word ☆ _____.

Use the –ar– words from the list below to complete the Bible verses.

sharper	star	marble	garlic
garment	marred	market	hardness
martyrs	harden	harmless	marvel

1. "The word of God is quick, and powerful, and _____ than any twoedged sword..." Hebrews 4:12

2. "...of brass, and iron, and _____." Rev. 18:12

3. "Be ye...wise as serpents, and _____ as doves." Matt. 10:16

4. "For we have seen his _____ in the east..." Matt. 2:2

5. "Being grieved for the _____ of their hearts..." Mark 3:5

6. "He disputed daily in the _____ with them..." Acts 17:17

7. "_____ not...if the world hate you." 1John 3:13

8. "And I saw the woman drunken...with the blood of the _____ of Jesus..." Revelation 17:6

9. "His visage was so _____ more than any man." Is. 52:14

10. "_____ not your heart..." Psalm 95:8

11. "They saw a...man...clothed in a long white _____" Mk. 16:5

12. "We remember the fish which we did eat in Egypt freely; the cucumbers, and the melons, and the leeks, and the onions, and the _____." Numbers 11:5

Day 85

> **Clue:** When a word ends with a syllable that sounds like **-cher**, it is usually spelled with a **-ture**. For exceptions, see the note in the back of the book.

Correctly spell each of the words in the chart below by replacing the –cher with a **-ture**.

punccher _____	rapcher _____
legislacher _____	denchers _____
furnicher _____	leccher _____
miniacher _____	feacherd _____
literacher _____	advencher _____

Use the words, spelled correctly, from the chart above to fill in the blanks below.

1. My grandmother left her _____ in a cup to soak.

2. That tiny dog is called a _____ poodle.

3. Classics by Mark Twain are considered to be among some of America's greatest works of _____.

4. The event where followers of Christ will meet him in the "air" is commonly called the _____.

5. We attended a _____ on the Creation versus Evolution debate.

6. The _____ flavor was Double Fudge Ripple.

7. That broken glass in the road will _____ someone's tire.

8. It took us two days to move all the _____ to the new house.

Day 86

Clue: When a word ends with a syllable that sounds like **-cher**, it is usually spelled with a -_____. For exceptions, see the note in the back of the book.

Complete the puzzle using words ending with – ture.

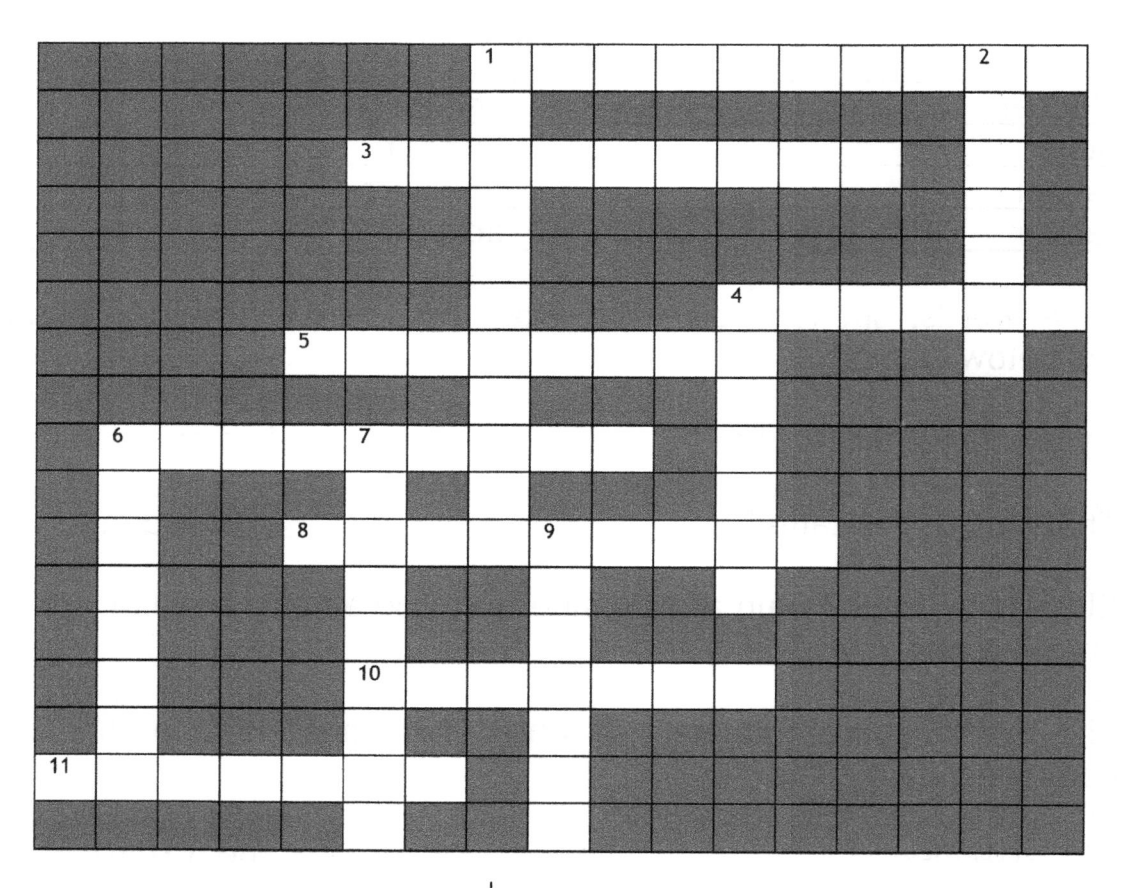

Across
1. Books; classics.
3. Your name or John Hancock.
4. Past, present, and _____.
5. A living thing; monster.
6. Table, chairs, beds.
8. An action-packed event.
10. Inflict excruciating pain.
11. Speech.

Down
1. The Senate and the House.
2. When Believers are gone, in the twinkling of an eye, with Jesus.
4. The *showcased* flavor or film.
6. A broken bone.
7. Contractual slavery.
9. To lovingly raise.

(Answers in alphabetical order: adventure, creature, feature, fracture, furniture, future, indenture, lecture, legislature, literature, nurture, rapture, signature, torture.)

Day 87

> **Clue:** When a word ends with a syllable that sounds like **-cher**, it is usually spelled with a -_____. For exceptions, see the note in the back of the book.

Correctly spell each of the words in the chart so that they end with -*ture*.

torcherd _____	nurcher _____	pascher _____
picchers _____	Scripcher _____	creacher _____
nacher _____	furnicher _____	fucher _____

Complete the verses below with correctly-spelled words from the chart.

1. "...the Tent of Meeting, the ark of the Testimony with the atonement cover on it, and all the other _____..." Exodus 31:7

2. "Know that the LORD is God. It is he who made us, and we are his; we are his people, the sheep of his _____." Ps. 100:3

3. "A word aptly spoken is like apples of gold in _____ of silver." Proverbs 25:11

4. "For I know the thoughts that I think toward you...thoughts of peace and not of evil, to give you a _____ and a hope." Jer. 29:11

5. "Go into all the world and preach the gospel to every _____." Mk. 16:15.

6. "Do not provoke your children to wrath, but bring them up in the _____ and admonition of the Lord." Ephesians 6:4

7. "All _____ is given by inspiration of God..." 2 Tim. 3:16

8. "Others were_____, not accepting deliverance." Heb. 11:35

9. "...You may be partakers of the divine_____." 2 Pet. 1:4

Day 88

> **Clue:** When a word ends with a syllable that sounds like **-cher**, it is usually spelled with a -_____. For exceptions, see the note in the back of the book.

Correctly spell each of the words in the chart so that they end with *-ture*.

tinccher _____	indencher _____	macher _____
miniacher _____	feacherd _____	literacher _____
fixcher _____	advenchers _____	
sucher _____	deparcher _____	

Complete these sentences with correctly-spelled words from the chart:

1. We had many _____ when we went to Ocean City for vacation.

2. Our vacation _____ several unusual happenings and even mishaps.

3. It rained so much, I guess you could say that bad weather was a _____ for that vacation.

4. While fishing, the boys accidentally hooked a fully- _____ sea gull by the wing.

5. Though it would have been nice to _____ the wound and put _____ of iodine on it, the large, frantic bird would allow no such thing!

6. Between rain storms, the ground around our campsite was crawling with _____ crabs, no bigger around than a quarter.

7. There were many other adventures, most of them enjoyable, and the time of our _____ brought sadness.

Day 89

Clue: When a word ends with a syllable that sounds like *-cher*, it is usually spelled with a -_____. For exceptions, see the note in the back of the book.

There are nine misspelled *-ture* words in the story below. Circle them, then write them correctly on the lines below.

    William Penn was a great man of God. He lived in a time when Christians were commonly torchered for their faith. He himself became a Christian as a youth. Once he made the commitment to follow God, his life was never the same. He just moved from one advencher to another.
    Penn, a lawyer, spent much of his life defending Christians in court. In those days macher Christians would rather die for their faith than deny Christ. The English legislacher had already passed laws allowing the people the right to a fair trial, but few courts of that day practiced the law, especially when it came to Christians. Penn was determined to fight for this right – and he was thrown into prison for his pains.
    Actually, Penn wasn't a stranger to prison. He had been capchered and thrown in prison a number of times for preaching the gospel. He gave up much more, though, than just his freedom for the sake of the gospel. His father, the Admiral, hounded him much of his life to give up his religion. The Admiral lecchered him, threatened him, and even disinherited him. Penn actually came from a very wealthy family that held high position in the King's court, but he gave it all up for Jesus.
    Eventually the Lord led William Penn to establish a colony where the government was based on Scripcher. The King of England himself placed his signacher on the charter that granted Penn that vast wilderness territory that we know today as Pennsylvania. In this new colony, Christians would finally be able to live in peace, to practice their faith freely, and to offer their children a fucher full of hope.

_____   _____   _____
_____   _____   _____
_____   _____   _____

Day 90 – Review

Clue: Memorize this poem: "___ before ___ except after ___, or when it says ___ as in neighbor and weigh." This means that in words with this vowel combination...
- If the letter c is first, use a -_____.
- If the word has the long a sound, use -_____.
- The above two are uncommon, so mostly you will use an -_____.

Clue: How do you keep the words *was*, *want*, and *what* straight?
- _____ is the past tense of the word *is*. The "uh" sound is spelled with an __, and there is no -__-. It is a short word, just like all of the "be" verbs.
- _____ means *desire*. It does not have an -__, nor an apostrophe. Remember: You _____ always have what you_____.
- _____ is one of the "5 w's" (who, _____, where, when, and why). All "5 w's" begin with "____".

Clue: When the letters -_____- are blended together, they form the sound that you hear in the word ☆ _____.

Clue: When a word ends with a syllable that sounds like *-cher*, it is usually spelled with a -_____. For exceptions, see the note in the back of the book.

Using the clues above, complete the sentences below.

1. _____ (wut) is the name of the _____ (type of vehicle) that is played by a Volkswagen in the movies?

2. The _____ (Scripchers) say that we must _____ (beleeve) in the name of Jesus if we _____(wunt) to be saved.

3. That _____ (immacher) child s_____ (another word for "began") jumping on the _____ (furnicher) as soon as he thought he _____ (wuz) alone.

4. The recipe c_____ (name for small, stiff sheet of paper) showed a big _____ (peece) of pie that was sure to appeal to our gluttonous _____ (nachers).

Day 91

> **Clue:** These words have tricky spellings, but they are commonly used. Memorize their spellings.
> - "Any" and "many" rhyme. The short -e sound is spelled with an -a.
> - "Already" is one word that sounds like a compound word (all + ready); however, there is only one -l in this word.
> - "Sure" sounds like it starts with an -sh; however, it is spelled with just an -s. You can remember it like this: "I <u>s</u>ure like <u>s</u>ugar after <u>s</u>upper!"

Circle the misspelled words in the sentences below, and write them correctly on the lines provided.

1. Does enyone know where Maple Avenue is? _____

2. It's only 9:00 AM, and it's all ready 88° outside! _____

3. It shore is hot today! _____

4. When Grandpa asked, "Would enyone like to ride with me?," I said, "Shore! I would." _____ _____

5. I have all ready found mennie Bible verses to help you with your spelling. _____ _____

6. I shore don't want eny rain this weekend! _____ _____

7. Can you believe that it's all ready 3:00? _____

8. Meny times I have prayed for my children's safety. _____

9. Are you shore that you want your hair cut in that fashion? _____

10. How menny cavities do you have? _____

11. The children are all ready in bed. _____

12. Are you shore you don't want enny ice cream? _____ _____

13. We've picked meny berries all ready. _____ _____

Day 92

> **Clue:** These words have tricky spellings, but they are commonly used. Memorize their spellings.
> - "Any" and "many"_____. The short –e sound is spelled with an ___.
> - "Already" is _____word that sounds like a compound word (all + ready); however, there is only _____ ___in this word.
> - "Sure" sounds like it starts with an -_____; however, it is spelled with just an ___. Remember it like this: "I ___re like ___gar after ___pper!"

Complete the sentences below using *any, many, already,* and *sure.*

1. How _____ of you enjoy going to the dentist?

2. She is only three months old and _____ she has four teeth.

3. That library _____ does have _____ books for kids!

4. Our library hardly has _____ kids' books.

5. I would rather not have _____ gravy on my rice, thank you.

6. Are you _____ you put Dad's shovel away when you were through? He can't find it _____where.

7. We _____ looked all over the garage for it.

8. You put too _____ fries on her plate. She'll eat hardly _____ of them.

9. We're _____ done school for the day!

10. I _____ love Christmas vacation!

11. I am _____ I remembered to lock the door.

12. He doesn't have _____ money left over for souvenirs.

13. There are too _____ kids riding in this van.

Day 93

Clue: These words have tricky spellings, but they are commonly used. Memorize their spellings.
- "Any" and "many"_____. The short -e sound is spelled with an ___.
- "Already" is _____word that sounds like a compound word (all + ready); however, there is only _____ ___in this word.
- "Sure" sounds like it starts with an -_____; however, it is spelled with just an ___. Remember it like this: "I ___re like ___gar after ___pper!"

Complete the Bible passages with the words *any, many, already* and *sure*.

1. "...Behold, I lay in Zion for a foundation a stone, a tried stone, a precious corner stone, a _____ foundation..." Isaiah 28:16

2. "I praised the dead which are _____ dead..." Ecc. 4:2

3. "And see if there be _____ wicked way in me..." Psalm 139:24

4. "His feet like unto fine brass, as if they burned in a furnace; and his voice as the sound of _____ waters." Rev. 1:15

5. "Lift up your eyes, and look on the fields; for they are white _____ to harvest." John 4:35

6. "He that believeth on him is not condemned: but he that believeth not is condemned _____." John 3:18

7. "As _____ as I love, I rebuke and chasten." Rev. 3:19

8. "I will sing praises to my God while I have _____ being."Ps. 146:2

9. "For as we have _____ members in one body..." Rom. 12:4

10. "Be ye _____ of this, that the kingdom of God is come nigh unto you." Luke 10:11

11. "Be _____ your sin will find you out." Numbers 32:23

12. "They that seek the Lord shall not want _____good thing."Ps.34:10

Day 94

> **Clue:** These words have tricky spellings, but they are commonly used. Memorize their spellings.
> - "Any" and "many" _____. The short –e sound is spelled with an ___.
> - "Already" is _____ word that sounds like a compound word (all + ready); however, there is only _____ ___ in this word.
> - "Sure" sounds like it starts with an -_____; however, it is spelled with just an ___. Remember it like this: "I ___re like ___gar after ___pper!"

1. "There shall no evil befall thee, neither shall _____ plague come nigh thy dwelling." Psalm 91:10

2. "Not as though I had _____ attained, either were _____ perfect: but I follow after…" Philippians 3:12

3. …Testimony of the Lord is_____, making wise the simple. Ps.19:7

4. "I heard the voice of _____ angels round the throne." Rev.5:11

5. "As _____ as are led by the Spirit of God, they are the sons of God." Romans 8:14

6. "That he might be the firstborn among _____ brethren." Ro.8:29

7. "No man is _____ of life." Job 24:22

8. "When Jesus came, he found that he had lain in the grave four days _____." John 11:17

9. "He shall give his angels charge over thee: in their hands they shall bear thee up, lest at _____ time thou dash thy foot…" Matt. 4:6

10. "That which hath been is named _____." Ecc. 6:10

11. "The foundation of God standeth _____." 2 Tim. 2:19

12. If _____ man will come after me, let him deny himself, and take up his cross, and follow me." Matthew 16:24

Day 95

Clue: If a *short-vowel* word or syllable *ends* with a -j sound, the -j sound is usually spelled with a -dge.

Spell the words in the chart correctly, then use them, spelled correctly, to complete the sentences below.

ej	plej	juj
drej	gruj	loj
hej	fuj	nuj

1. In a marriage ceremony, you _____ yourself to another 'til death parts you.

2. A _____ presides over a trial, which is conducted before a jury of peers.

3. A rich, chocolate treat that tastes good when heated and poured over ice cream is called _____.

4. In the pinewood derby race, each boy had to give his car a small _____ to get it going as the signal sounded.

5. Another name for a cabin or dwelling in the woods is a _____.

6. Bushes and plants that form a barrier between two areas are known as a _____.

7. When a river bottom gets clogged with debris, workers can _____ it to clear it.

8. If I stand too close to the _____ of a steep cliff, I get very dizzy.

9. When someone offends you, and you stay angry at that person, that is called "holding a _____."

Day 96

Clue: If a _____-vowel word or syllable _____with a -___ sound, the -j sound is usually spelled with a -_____.

Fill in the blanks in the clues, then find the *-dge* words in the word-search puzzle below.

a	s	d	f	g	h	j	k	l	q	e	r	e	r	t	y	e	u	i
b	o	p	z	x	c	v	b	n	q	a	e	r	g	t	g	y	u	o
u	i	a	s	d	f	g	e	h	j	k	l	z	x	d	c	v	b	n
d	q	e	r	t	t	e	g	d	i	M	y	u	i	i	e	o	p	a
g	s	d	f	g	h	j	d	k	l	z	x	r	c	g	v	b	n	q
e	e	r	t	y	u	i	a	o	p	a	b	s	a	d	f	g	h	j
t	k	l	z	x	c	v	b	b	n	q	e	d	r	t	y	u	i	o
p	a	s	d	f	g	h	j	k	l	z	g	z	s	l	e	d	g	e
x	h	o	d	g	e	p	o	d	g	e	c	v	M	b	n	q	e	r
t	y	u	r	i	o	p	a	r	t	s	d	f	u	g	h	j	k	l
z	x	c	e	v	b	n	q	u	e	r	t	y	d	u	i	o	p	a
s	d	f	d	g	h	j	k	d	l	z	x	c	g	v	b	n	q	e
r	t	y	g	u	i	o	p	g	r	u	d	g	e	a	s	d	f	g
h	j	k	e	l	z	x	c	e	c	v	b	n	q	e	r	t	y	u

Clues:

1. A policeman wears this:_____
2. One who does hard work: _____
3. Financial planning:_____
4. To clear a river bottom:_____
5. A type of hammer:_____
6. A very short person:_____
7. Gizmo:_____
8. Staying angry:_____
9. Mish-mash:_____
10. Border:_____
11. Smear:_____
12. Spans water:_____

(Use these words: badge, bridge, budget, dredge, drudge, edge, gadget, grudge, hodgepodge, midget, sledge, smudge)

Day 97

Clue: If a _____-vowel word or syllable _____ with a -___ sound, the -j sound is usually spelled with a -_____.

Spell the words in the chart correctly, then use them, spelled correctly, to complete the sentences below.

wej	lej	sluj
slej	buj	baj
puj	brij	gajet

1. When the old mule dug in his heels, we couldn't make him _____ an inch.

2. When I saw we were having pecan pie for dessert, I asked for a large _____ of it.

3. During the spring rains, the small _____ over Indian Creek is often flooded.

4. After the shipping accident, the waters of the bay were covered with a thick, oily _____.

5. Since he was only two, little Bobby hadn't lost his baby _____ yet. He was still round and dimpled.

6. Chris has an interesting _____. It unfolds into several tools, utensils, and even a comb – all in one!

7. We needed to use a _____ hammer to break up the old sidewalk.

8. As the school's director of discipline, my grandmother was given a _____ that looked like one a policeman would wear.

9. We sat on a _____ of Signal Mountain and watched fireworks over the Tennessee Valley.

Day 98

> **Clue:** If a _____-vowel word or syllable _____ with a -___ sound, the -j sound is usually spelled with a -_____.

Spell the words in the chart correctly, then use them, spelled correctly, to complete the Bible verses below. Some words are used several times.

bajr	ej	gruj
hej	juj	lejs
plej	loj	wej

1. "The LORD shall _____ the peoples; _____ me, O LORD, according to my righteousness..." Psalm 7:8

2. "And they will fall by the _____ of the sword, and be led away captive into all nations." Luke 21:24

3. "_____ not one against another, brethren, lest you be condemned..." James 5:9

4. "Have you not made a _____ around him, around his household, and around all that he has on every side?" Job 1:10

5. "Wherever you go, I will go; and wherever you _____, I will _____; Your people shall be my people, and your God, my God." Ruth 1:16

6. "You shall not pervert justice due the stranger or the fatherless, nor take a widow's garment as a _____." Deut. 24:17

7. "Over the golden altar they shall spread a blue cloth, and cover it with a covering of _____ skins..." Numbers 4:11

8. Concerning the temple of the Lord: "And on the borders that were between the _____ were lions, oxen, and cherubims: and upon the _____ there was a base above..." 1 Kings 7:29

9. "When I saw among the spoils a beautiful Babylonian garment, 200 shekels of silver, and a _____ of gold weighing 50 shekels, I coveted them and took them." Joshua 7:21

Day 99

Clue: If a _____-*vowel* word or syllable _____ with a -____ sound, the -j sound is usually spelled with a -_____.

Circle the misspelled words in the sentences and spell them correctly on the lines following.

1. It only took a nuj to roll the large boulder over the ej of the cliff.
_____ _____

2. The inside of the loj was decorated with a hojpoj of Indian artifacts and antique farm implements. _____ _____

3. The Bible tells us we shouldn't juj one another, nor should we hold a gruj. _____ _____

4. Purchasing a $700 mijet racer so Josh could enter the tournament simply wasn't in the bujet. _____ _____

5. The engineers had to drej the river under the brij so that the ships could pass. _____ _____

6. Please pour some fuj over my wej of s'more pie. _____
_____

7. Since so many groundhogs dug holes under the hej and got into the garden, we had to get a special gajet to trap them.
_____ _____

8. The protesters refused to buj from the front of the clinic until they saw the policeman's baj. _____ _____

9. After working all day to remove the sluj from the oil spill, you'll have to be careful not to smuj the car's upholstery on your way home.
_____ _____

Day 100 Review

Clue: Words that end with a long -i sound plus -t are usually spelled with an _____. The -_____ is silent.

Clue: The words "because" and "before" both begin with a _____ and end with a silent _____.

    • _____ has an -aw- sound that is spelled with an -_____-.
    • _____ has the word "_____" in the middle
The words "always" and "almost" both begin with an _____-.
    • _____ ends with the word "_____."
    • _____ ends with the word "_____."

Clue: These words have tricky spellings, but they are commonly used. Memorize their spellings.

    • "Any" and "many"_____. The short -e sound is spelled with an ___.
    • "Already" is _____word that sounds like a compound word (all + ready); however, there is only _____ ___in this word.
    • "Sure" sounds like it starts with an -_____; however, it is spelled with just an ___. Remember it like this: "I ___re like ___gar after ___pper!"

Clue: If a *short-vowel* word or syllable ends with a -j sound, the -j sound is usually spelled with a -_____.

Using the clues provided, fill in the blanks in the sentences below.

1. _____ (Menny) people were brought from darkness into the glorious _____ (lite) of the Gospel _____ (becuz) of the courage of the missionaries.

2. They _____ (all most) _____ (all ways) remembered to brush their teeth _____ (be + 4) bed, so they didn't have _____ (ennie) cavities.

3. They were so _____ (shure) their preparations were adequate that they had _____ (all ready) left camp to climb the mountain _____ (be + 4) it was even _____ (brite) enough to see.

4. We _____ (fite) the enemy with a two- _____ (ejed) sword, yet God has _____ (hejd) us about with His protection.

Day 101

Clue: The sound that you hear when you say 4 (f-o-u-r) is usually spelled:
- With an **-or** if the word ends with a consonant (as in *fort*), or..
- With an **-ore** if the word ends with the –r sound (as in *more*).

Fill in the blanks with –or words. (cord, Ford, horse, Lord, porch, pork, short, sports, stork, storms, thorns, torn)

1. A long, rubber-encased wire with plugs at either end is called an electric _____.

2. Basketball, baseball, soccer, tennis, and gymnastics are all _____.

3. The Mustang, the Model T, and the Explorer are all cars manufactured by _____.

4. Hurricanes, blizzards, and nor'easters are all types of bad weather called _____.

5. The sharp, pointy projections that cover the stems of roses and raspberry bushes are called _____.

6. People who are small in stature are said to be _____.

7. Jesus is our savior. He should also be our king or _____.

8. Bacon, chops, sausage, and scrapple are examples of meat from pigs called _____.

9. A large bird that reportedly delivers babies to waiting families is called a _____.

10. A roofed platform built onto the front of a house where people enjoy sitting in the evenings is called a _____.

11. A beautiful animal ridden by cowboys and Indians (hint: this word ends with a silent -e): _____.

12. Another word for "ripped." _____

Day 102

Clue: The sound that you hear when you say 4 (f-o-u-r) is usually spelled:
- With an -____ if the word ends with a _____(as in *fort*), or..
- With an -_____ if the word ends with the -____ sound (as in *more*).

Fill in the puzzle with –or words by completing the clues below, using: *dories, force, fork, horn, horse, Jordan, morning, north, ore, scorn, short, sports, stories, thorn, torn, vortex.*

Across
3. Metal mixed with rock.
4. Knife, _____, and spoon.
6. Opposite of evening.
7. Fables; tales.
9. Pricker on a rose.
11. Small boats.
13. River where Jesus was baptized.
14. Pony; stallion.

Down
1. Trumpet, bugle, etc.
2. Ripped.
4. Navy, Army, Marines, Air _____.
5. Center of a tornado.
7. Mockery; contempt.
8. Baseball, soccer, tennis, track, etc.
10. Not south.
12. Not tall.

Day 103

Clue: The sound that you hear when you say 4 (f-o-u-r) is usually spelled:
- With an -____ if the word ends with a _____(as in *fort*), or..
- With an -_____ if the word ends with the -___ sound (as in *more*).

Fill in the sentences with –or words. (Use these words: cord, core, forms, Lord, more, nor, North, or, platform, record, report, shore, sore, story)

1. The boat washed up on the sea_____.

2. The center of the apple is called the apple _____.

3. A sunburn can make your skin very tender and _____.

4. These conjunctions work together: either- _____, and neither-_____.

5. In the public schools, your grades are displayed on a quarterly _____ card.

6. If you have an answering machine, you can _____ your telephone messages when you are away.

7. Shoes with thick, chunky soles that raise your height several inches are called _____ shoes.

8. Jesus is _____!

9. The opposite of less is _____.

10. The boys enjoy it when I tell them a _____ from my childhood.

11. Each year we must fill out tax _____ and turn them in by April 15th.

12. Santa Claus supposedly lives at the _____ Pole.

13. Jason taped down the electric _____ so no one would trip over it.

Day 104

Clue: The sound that you hear when you say 4 (f-o-u-r) is usually spelled:
- With an -____ if the word ends with a _____(as in *fort)*, or..
- With an -_____ if the word ends with the -____ sound (as in *more*).

Complete these Bible verses with –or words. Use these words: before, born, conformed, exhort, for, glory, horse, Jordan, Lord (4 X), morning (2 X), stork, storm, sword, thorns, transformed.

1. "I will sing unto the _____, for he hath triumphed gloriously: the _____ and rider hath he thrown into the sea." Ex. 15:1

2. "Every tongue should confess that Jesus Christ is _____ to the _____ of God the Father.

3. "Behold, the ark of the covenant of the _____ of all the earth passeth over _____ you into the _____." Josh. 3:11

4. "My voice shalt thou hear in the _____, O _____; in the _____ will I direct my prayer unto thee…" Psalm 5:4

5. "_____ the word of God is quick, and powerful, and sharper than any two-edged _____…" Hebrews 4:12

6. "And there arose a great _____ of wind, and the waves beat into the ship, so that it was now full." Mark 4:37

7. "As for the _____, the fir trees are her house." Psalm 104:17

8. "Then Pilate therefore took Jesus, and scourged him. And the soldiers platted a crown of _____, and put it on his head, and they put on him a purple robe…" John 19:1-2

9. "But _____ one another daily, while it is called Today." Heb. 3:13

10. "And be not _____ to this world: but be ye _____ by the renewing of your mind…" Romans 12:2

11. "And he is the head of the body, the church: who is the beginning, the first_____ from the dead….." Colossians 1:18

Day 105

Clue: The following words are tricky and need to be memorized since they don't follow the rules. Each of them has just one vowel: an -o.
- *Do* rhymes with 2. (The past tense, *done*, rhymes with *fun*.)
- *Who* has a silent -w. It also rhymes with *two* (which also has a silent -w.)
- *Of* rhymes with *love*. The -o sounds like a -u, and the -f sounds like a -v.
- *Only* has a long -o sound.

Use the words *do*, *who*, *of*, and *only* in the sentences below:

1. What _____ you want to _____ today?

2. "If I _____ had a brain," sang the scarecrow in the *Wizard of Oz*.

3. This is Monica Grace _____ Philadelphia, Pennsylvania.

4. _____ is responsible for closing the gates?

5. Uh-oh! We _____ have one cup _____ flour left to make a cake.

6. _____ _____ you think you are?

7. He is the lily _____ the valley.

8. Get out _____ there quick!

9. I have no idea _____ broke the mirror.

10. There are _____ two girls in his Sunday School class.

11. _____ you remember which _____ these were still valid?

12. You were _____ supposed to _____ two pages today.

13. _____ would like a cup _____ coffee?

14. It's too early to get up. It's _____ 6:30 in the morning.

15. I know _____ did such a good job with the dishes today.

Day 106

Clue: The following words are tricky and need to be memorized since they don't follow the rules. Each of them has just one vowel: an _____.
- _____ rhymes with 2. (The past tense, _____, rhymes with *fun*.)
- *Who* has a silent -____. It also rhymes with ____ (which also has a silent -w.)
- ____ rhymes with *love*. The -__ sounds like a -u, and the -__ sounds like a -v.
- *Only* has a long -____ sound.

Use *do*, *doing*, *done*, *of*, *who*, and *only* to complete the verses from the Sermon on the Mount in the gospel of Matthew.

1. "Blessed are those _____ mourn, for they will be comforted." 5:4

2. "Blessed are those _____ hunger and thirst for righteousness, for they will be filled." 5:6

3. "Blessed are those _____ are persecuted because _____ righteousness, for theirs is the kingdom of heaven." 5:10

4. "Anyone _____ breaks one _____ the least _____ these commandments and teaches other to _____ the same will be called least in the kingdom _____ heaven." 5:10

5. "_____ not break your oath, but keep the oaths you have made to the Lord." 5:33

6. "Love your enemies and pray for those _____ persecute you, that you may be sons _____ your Father in heaven." 5:44-45

7. "If you love those _____ love you, what reward will you get?...And if you greet _____ your brothers, what are you _____ more than others? _____ not even pagans ____ that?" 5:46-47

8. "When you give to the needy, _____ not let your left hand know what your right hand is _____,...Then your Father, _____ sees what is _____ in secret, will reward you." 6:3

9. "Your kingdom come, your will be _____...." 6:10

Day 107

Clue: The following words are tricky and need to be memorized since they don't follow the rules. Each of them has just one vowel: an _____.
- _____ rhymes with *2*. (The past tense, _____, rhymes with *fun*.)
- *Who* has a silent -____. It also rhymes with ____ (which also has a silent -w.)
- ____ rhymes with *love*. The -__ sounds like a -u, and the -__ sounds like a -v.
- *Only* has a long -____ sound.

Use *do*, *of*, *who*, and *only* to complete the verses from the Sermon on the Mount and the eighth chapter of the gospel of Matthew.

1. "But when you fast...wash your face, so that it will not be obvious to men that you are fasting, but _____ to your Father..." 6:17-18

2. "The eye is the lamp ____ the body." 6:22

3. "In everything, _____ to others what you would have them _____ to you..." 7:12

4. "Not everyone _____ says to me, 'Lord, Lord,' will enter the kingdom _____ heaven, but _____ he _____ does the will ____ my Father _____ is in heaven." 7:21

5. "Therefore everyone _____ hears these words ____ mine and puts them into practice is like a man _____ built his house on the rock." 7:24

6. "But everyone _____ hears these words _____ mine and does not put them into practice is like a foolish man _____ built his house on sand." 7:26

7. "He taught as one _____ had authority, and not as their teachers _____ the law." 7:29

8. "You _____ little faith, why are you so afraid?" 8:26

9. "What _____ you want with us, Son ____ God?" 8:29

Day 108

> **Clue:** The following words are tricky and need to be memorized since they don't follow the rules. Each of them has just one vowel: an _____.
> - _____ rhymes with 2. (The past tense, _____, rhymes with *fun*.)
> - *Who* has a silent -____. It also rhymes with ____ (which also has a silent -w.)
> - ____ rhymes with *love*. The -__ sounds like a -u, and the -__ sounds like a -v.
> - *Only* has a long -____ sound.

Circle the misspelled words in the sentences below and write them correctly on the lines following.

1. Which uv these dew you want to wear today? _____ _____

2. How many uf these doo you want me to sell? _____ _____

3. Hoo ownley took one piece? _____ _____

4. Whoe would like another piece? _____

5. The onley thing you can dew is pray. _____ _____

6. Doo you hear hoo is calling you? _____ _____

7. My little sister is the ownley one whoe is afraid uv the dark.
_____ _____ _____

8. Which uv you would rather have onley the chocolate one? _____
_____

9. There is ownly two uv these left. _____ _____

10. Doo you know which ov these can be frozen? _____ _____

11. How dew you doo? _____ _____

12. Some ov these fish are onely an inch long. _____ _____

Day 109

Clue: The following words are tricky and need to be memorized since they don't follow the rules. Each of them has just one vowel: an _____.
- _____ rhymes with *2*. (The past tense, _____, rhymes with *fun*.)
- *Who* has a silent -____. It also rhymes with ____ (which also has a silent -w.)
- ____ rhymes with *love*. The -__ sounds like a -u, and the -__ sounds like a -v.
- *Only* has a long -____ sound.

Fill in the Proverbs with the words *of*, *who*, *do*, and *only*.

1. "He _____ brings trouble on his family will inherit _____ wind." 11:29

2. "The fruit _____ the righteous is a tree _____ life, and he _____ wins souls is wise." 11:30

3. "Truthful lips endure forever but a lying tongue lasts _____ a moment." 12:19

4. "The Lord detests lying lips, but he delights in men _____ are truthful." 12:22

5. "He _____ spares the rod hates his son, but he _____ loves him is careful to discipline him." 13:24

6. "Commit to the LORD whatever you _____, and your plans will succeed." 16:3

7. "Gray hair is a crown _____ splendor." 16:31

8. "The name _____ the LORD is a strong tower." 18:10

9. "_____ not let your heart envy sinners, but always be zealous for the fear _____ the LORD." 23:17

10. "He _____ works his land will have abundant food, but the one _____ chases fantasies will have his fill _____ poverty." 28:19

Day 110 Review

Clue: The sound that you hear when you say 4 (f-o-u-r) is usually spelled:
- With an -____ if the word ends with a _____ (as in *fort*), or..
- With an -_____ if the word ends with the -___ sound (as in *more*).

Clue: The following words are tricky and need to be memorized since they don't follow the rules. Each of them has just one vowel: an _____.
- _____ rhymes with *2*. (The past tense, _____, rhymes with *fun*.)
- *Who* has a silent -____. It also rhymes with ____ (which also has a silent -w.)
- ____ rhymes with *love*. The -__ sounds like a -u, and the -__ sounds like a -v.
- *Only* has a long -____ sound.

Clue: When the letters -_____- are blended together, they form the sound that you hear in the word ⭐ _____.

Clue: When a word ends with a syllable that sounds like -*cher*, it is usually spelled with a -_____. See the note in the back of this book.

Fill in the blanks with words using the clues in the parentheses.

1. Which _____ (uv) these _____ (picchers) _____ (dew) you think we should sell at the _____ (f_____mer's) _____ (m____ket)?

2. There is _____ (ownley) one person _____ (hoo) would know how to get out _____ (uv) the boat, walk on water, and even calm the _____ (st__m).

3. _____ (doo) you think you'll win a place on the police _____ (f__ce) if you _____ (capcher) the thief?

4. In the _____ (m__ning), _____ (hoo) would like to hike to the mouth _____ (uv) the _____ (J____dan) River, and _____ (hoo) would rather visit the _____ (g__den) _____ (uv) Gethsemane?

Day 111

Clue: The long -a sound is usually spelled one of three ways. These spellings must be memorized:
- With an *-ai*.
- With an *-a* followed by a *silent -e* on the end.
- If the word *ends* with the long -a sound, it is usually spelled with an *-ay*.

Fill in the following clues with *long-a-silent-e* words.

ace	ate	bake
cake	games	grace
grade	grape	late
made	names	sale

1. If you aren't on time, you are _____.

2. In a deck of cards, this card often has the highest value: _____

3. Why did God choose you, call you, and redeem you? Because of His _____.

4. When a family sets their unwanted belongings in the yard for the community to purchase, it is called a yard _____.

5. When dried, this fruit is called a raisin: _____

6. If you built a model of a ship, that is what you _____.

7. If you got a "C" on your math test, that is your _____.

8. If you consumed fruit and cereal for breakfast, that is what you _____.

9. If it is someone's birthday, you will need to _____ a _____.

10. Uno, hopscotch, Monopoly, and tag are all _____ of _____.

Day 112

Clue: The long -a sound is usually spelled one of three ways. These spellings must be memorized:
- With an -____ as in **train**.
- With an -__ followed by a *silent* -____ on the end, as in **save**.
- If the word *ends* with the long -a sound, it is usually spelled with an -____.

Fill in the following clues with **long-a-silent-e** words.

base	females	flame
hate	males	page
place	planes	safe
save	share	stage

1. A tongue of fire is called a _____

2. Jets, gliders, and Cessnas are all types of _____.

3. When you want to give half of your candy bar to your brother, you want to _____.

4. In baseball you run to first, second, and third _____.

5. If you make it to third base without being tagged, you are _____.

6. Jesus didn't come to condemn the world, but to _____ the world.

7. The opposite of love is _____.

8. Each separate sheet of paper that makes up a book is called a _____.

9. The first person to cross the finish line came in first _____.

10. An actor acts on a _____.

11. Boys and girls are also called _____ and _____.

Day 113

Clue: The long –a sound is usually spelled one of three ways. These spellings must be memorized:
- With an -____ as in **train**.
- With an -__ followed by a *silent* -____ on the end, as in **save**.
- If the word *ends* with the long –a sound, it is usually spelled with an -____.

Complete these clues with long *-ai* words.

bail	chair	failed
hail	hair	mail
nail	paid	pair
plain	raid	sail

1. If you sent money to the electric and phone companies, then your bills are _____.

2. If your boat is filling with water, you'll have to _____ it.

3. If you are going to eat all the goodies out of the refrigerator, you are going to _____ it.

4. If you got an "F" on your math test, you _____ it.

5. Ice balls that fall during a storm are called _____.

6. A boat that moves by wind being caught in large canvas triangles is called a _____ boat.

7. Every day the postman puts letters in your _____ box.

8. You sit on a _____.

9. Two socks are called a _____.

10. Your head is covered with _____.

11. With a hammer you hit the head of the _____.

12. If it's not very fancy, it is _____.

Day 114

> **Clue:** The long –a sound is usually spelled one of three ways. These spellings must be memorized:
> - With an -____ as in **train**.
> - With an -__ followed by a *silent* -____ on the end, as in **save**.
> - If the word *ends* with the long –a sound, it is usually spelled with an -____.

Complete these clues with long *-ai* words.

air	brain	claim
gain	jail	main
pain	rain	snail
Spain	trail	train

1. If you are in an accident, you must turn in an insurance _____.

2. Settlers heading west traveled the Oregon _____.

3. Criminals go to _____.

4. A slug-like creature with a shell on its back is a _____.

5. What you breathe: _____

6. If you ate three hot-fudge sundaes every day, you would _____ weight.

7. The same as *major* or *predominant*: _____

8. A form of precipitation: _____

9. The organ protected by your skull: _____

10. The country where people speak Spanish: _____

11. If you had a headache, you would feel _____ in your head.

12. This form of transportation runs on a track: _____.

Day 115

Clue: The long –a sound is usually spelled one of three ways. These spellings must be memorized:
- With an -____ as in **train**.
- With an -__ followed by a *silent* -____ on the end, as in **save**.
- If the word *ends* with the long –a sound, it is usually spelled with an -____.

Complete the following clues with long -*ay* words.

bay	day	gray
holidays	jay	pay
play	ray	say
stay	stray	way

1. Twenty-four hours equals one _____.

2. If you want to go to the circus, you must _____ for a ticket.

3. Another word for light black: _____

4. A beautiful bird with blue feathers is called a blue _____.

5. A dog or cat that wanders around and does not have an owner is called a _____.

6. A stream of light that comes from the sun is called a _____.

7. Christmas, Easter, and 4th of July are all _____.

8. If you couldn't hear what a person said, you might ask, "What did you _____?"

9. If given a choice, most kids would rather do this than do school: _____.

10. If you didn't want your dog to run off, you might command him to _____.

11. The place where the ocean curves into the land is called a _____.

12. Jesus is the _____.

Day 116

> **Clue:** The long –a sound is usually spelled one of three ways. These spellings must be memorized:
> - With an -____ as in **train**.
> - With an -__ followed by a **_silent_** -___ on the end, as in **save**.
> - If the word *ends* with the long –a sound, it is usually spelled with an -___.

Complete the following clues with long -*ay* words.

clay	cray	dismay
fray	gay	hay
Kay	May	pray
slay	sway	tray

1. A minor skirmish or battle is called a _____.

2. A girl's name: _____.

3. An old-fashioned word for happy is _____.

4. What the prince had to do to the mythical dragon: _____ it.

5. A month in spring: _____.

6. Horses eat this: _____.

7. God said that He is the potter and we are the _____.

8. When we speak to God, we _____.

9. If you wanted to feed your mother breakfast in bed, you would serve it on a _____ (which is a great idea, by the way).

10. If you climbed to the top of a tree, and the wind was blowing, you would feel the tree _____.

11. A small, fresh water creature that resembles a tiny lobster is called a _____ fish.

12. If you realized you were in big trouble, you would feel _____.

Day 117

Clue: The long -a sound is usually spelled one of three ways. These spellings must be memorized:
- With an -____ as in **train**.
- With an -__ followed by a *silent* -___ on the end, as in **save**.
- If the word *ends* with the long -a sound, it is usually spelled with an -___.

First, fill in the clues, then find the **long -a words** in the puzzle below using these words: *lakes, blue jay, tame, crate, remains, slate, scales, train, brain, saint, stain, holidays, pray.*

1. A bird. His feathers are a primary color. ____ ___
2. A type of box, usually wooden: _____.
3. Christmas, Thanksgiving, and Passover are all _____.
4. Erie, Superior, Huron, Michigan, and Ontario are the Great _____.
5. Talk to God: ____.
6. Left overs; stays behind: _____.
7. A person canonized in the Catholic Church. _____
8. You practice these on the piano. They cover a fish. _____.
9. What chalkboards and shingles used to be made of: _____.
10. If you slide on the grass, it will leave a green mark on your knees called a grass _____.
11. A domesticated or trained animal is considered to be ____.
12. This vehicle runs on a railroad: _____.
13. The organ protected by your skull: _____.

a	y	c	e	t	a	l	s	s	d	f	h
g	a	r	h	j	k	l	z	n	x	c	o
t	r	a	i	n	v	n	i	a	t	s	l
a	p	t	s	e	k	a	l	b	n	n	i
m	m	e	q	w	r	e	r	t	i	y	d
e	u	i	o	b	l	u	e	j	a	y	a
p	a	s	c	a	l	e	s	s	s	d	y
r	e	m	a	i	n	s	f	g	h	j	s

Day 118

> **Clue:** The long -a sound is usually spelled one of three ways. These spellings must be memorized:
> - With an -_____ as in **train**.
> - With an -___ followed by a *silent* -___ on the end, as in **save**.
> - If the word *ends* with the long -a sound, it is usually spelled with an -___.

Complete these Bible verses with **long -a** words.

behave	disgrace	face (2X)
faint	faith	gates
lame	name	place
pray	rain	shake

1. "He causes his sun to rise on the evil and the good, and sends _____ on the righteous and the unrighteous." Matt. 5:45

2. "On this rock I will build my church, and the _____ of hell will not prevail against it." Matthew 16:18

3. "For we will reap if we _____ not." Galatians 6:9

4. "The blind receive sight, the _____ walk, those who have leprosy are cured, the deaf hear..." Luke 7:22

5. "The apostles left the Sanhedrin, rejoicing because they had been counted worthy of suffering _____ for the _____." Acts 5:41

6. "Therefore I will make the heavens tremble; and the earth will _____ from its _____." Isaiah 13:13

7. Love... "doth not _____ itself unseemly." 1 Cor. 13:5

8. "For now we see through a glass, darkly; but then _____ to _____." 1 Corinthians 13:12

9. "_____ without ceasing." 1 Thessalonians 5:17

10. "The righteous will live by _____." Romans 1:17

Day 119

Clue: The long –a sound is usually spelled one of three ways. These spellings must be memorized:
- With an -____ as in **train**.
- With an -__ followed by a *silent* -____ on the end, as in **save**.
- If the word *ends* with the long –a sound, it is usually spelled with an -____.

Using the words in the word box to solve the clues, complete the following puzzle.

drape	fairy tale	lane
lemonade	mistake	parade
plate	prepay	scare
scrape	shave	snakes
snare	sprain spray	stale

Across
5. *Pinnochio* or *Sleeping Beauty*.
7. Take a stroll down memory ____.
9. To pay in advance.
10. An error.
11. An abrasion.
13. Used to trap a rabbit.
14. Floats and people march in a ___.
15. Remove whiskers.

Down
1. To squirt from a can.
2. Week-old bread is _____.
3. Dinner is served on a _____.
4. Rattlers, boas, and pythons.
6. A refreshing citrus drink.
8. To twist an ankle.
11. Frighten.
12. A curtain.

Day 120 Review

Clue: The long –a sound is usually spelled one of three ways. These spellings must be memorized:
- With an -____ as in **train**.
- With an -___ followed by a *silent* -____ on the end, as in **save**.
- If the word *ends* with the long –a sound, it is usually spelled with an -____.

Clue: Memorize this poem: "___ before ___ except after ___, or when it says ___ as in neighbor and weigh." This means that in words with this vowel combination…
- If the letter c is first, use a -_____.
- If the word has the long a sound, use -_____.
- The above two are uncommon, so mostly you will use an -_____.

Clue: These words have tricky spellings, but they are commonly used. Memorize their spellings.
- "Any" and "many"_____. The short –e sound is spelled with an ___.
- "Already" is _____word that sounds like a compound word (all + ready); however, there is only _____ ___in this word.
- "Sure" sounds like it starts with an -_____; however, it is spelled with just an ___. Remember it like this: "I ___re like ___gar after ___pper!"

Clue: If a short-*vowel* word or syllable ends with a -j sound, the -j sound is usually spelled with a -_____.

Using the clues, fill in the blanks in the sentences below.

1. It is my _____ (beleef) that if God were to _____ (juj) me for my works, I would _____ (fale), because my sins are _____ (meny).
2. But God doesn't hold _____(eny) of those sins against me since I have been _____ (saived) by _____ (graic) through _____ (fathe) in Jesus Christ.
3. He says that the _____ (feelds) are _____ (all + ready) white for harvest. This means _____ (meny) souls are on the _____ (ej) of eternal destruction and need to hear that the _____ (gaits) of heaven are open to all who will come.
4. We should _____ (prai) to the Lord of the harvest that he will _____ (rane) his Holy Spirit down on the hearts of men, that they will _____ (fante) not at troubles before them, and soon we will see Him _____ (faic) to _____ (faic).

Day 121

> **Clue:** The **long -o** sound in the *middle* of a word is usually spelled one of two ways:
> - An **-o** with a **silent -e** on the end (as in *hope*).
> - An **-oa** (as in *coat*).
>
> If the word **ends** with a **long -o** sound, it is usually spelled with an **-ow** (as in *snow*).
> Occasionally it is spelled with an **-o** (as in *go* and *no*) or an **-oe** (as in *toe*).

Fill in the blanks with **long-o-silent-e** words.

code	cone	chose
drone	drove	expose
hose	prone	rope
rose	slope	vote

1. An edible cup that holds ice cream is an ice-cream _____.

2. To reveal or bring to light is to _____.

3. If you readily catch colds, you are _____ to them.

4. A beautiful flower with thorns is a _____.

5. Past tense of choose: _____.

6. Dots and dashes make up the Morse _____.

7. We choose our president when we _____.

8. Heavy twisted cord used for mountain climbing is called _____.

9. Another name for a hill. What you ski down: _____.

10. This long, flexible tube waters your garden: _____.

11. Past tense of drive: _____.

12. A monotonous sound. A type of bee. _____.

Day 122

> **Clue:** The **long -o** sound in the *middle* of a word is usually spelled one of two ways:
> - An -___ with a **silent** -___ on the end (as in *hope*).
> - An -_____ (as in *coat*).
>
> If the word *ends* with a **long -o** sound, it is usually spelled with an -____ (as in *snow*).
> Occasionally it is spelled with an -___ (as in *go* and *no*) or an -_____ (as in *toe*).

Fill in the following clues with **long-o-silent-e** words.

bones	close	coke
dope	dove	hope
nose	phone	Pope
pose	scope	tote

1. What a skeleton is made of: _____.

2. The appendage that serves your sense of smell: _____.

3. This was invented by Alexander G. Bell: _____.

4. "These three things remain: faith, _____, and love."

5. These devices help us to see: tele- or micro_____.

6. A slang word for drugs: _____.

7. The head of the Catholic church. _____.

8. Opposite of open: _____.

9. To carry. Also a type of bag: _____.

10. A nickname for cola: _____.

11. What you do when you're having your picture taken: _____.

12. Past tense of dive: _____.

Day 123

Clue: The **long -o** sound in the *middle* of a word is usually spelled one of two ways:
- An -___ with a <u>silent</u> -___ on the end (as in *hope*).
- An -_____ (as in *coat*).

If the word *ends* with a **long -o** sound, it is usually spelled with an -____ (as in *snow*).
Occasionally it is spelled with an -__ (as in *go* and *no*) or an -_____ (as in *toe*).

Complete the clues with **long -oa** words.

bloat	boat	cloak
coal	coax	groan
load	loan	road
soak	soap	toad

1. To beg or entice is to _____.

2. A vehicle that travels on water: _____.

3. It cleans: _____.

4. A fuel: _____.

5. Borrowed money: _____.

6. A burden. To fill: _____.

7. A street or lane: _____.

8. Like a frog: _____.

9. To sit in water: _____.

10. A noise made in pain or sorrow: _____.

11. To swell or puff up: _____.

12. A cape or coat: _____.

Day 124

> **Clue:** The **long -o** sound in the *middle* of a word is usually spelled one of two ways:
> - An -___ with a **silent** -___ on the end (as in *hope*).
> - An -_____ (as in *coat*).
>
> If the word *ends* with a **long -o** sound, it is usually spelled with an -____ (as in *snow*).
> Occasionally it is spelled with an -___ (as in *go* and *no*) or an -_____ (as in *toe*).

Complete the clues with **long -oa** words.

boast	coast	coat
croak	foal	goal
moan	moat	oats
roast	throat	toast

1. Lightly browned bread: _____.

2. The back of your mouth and inside your neck: _____.

3. A jacket or cloak: _____.

4. A grain used for cereal: _____.

5. The sound a frog makes: _____.

6. A baby horse: _____.

7. A sound made when in pain: _____.

8. When you kick the soccer ball into the net, you've scored a _____.

9. Brag: _____.

10. Water surrounding a castle: _____.

11. Edge of a continent. Shore: _____.

12. To cook or bake: _____.

Day 125

Clue: The **long -o** sound in the *middle* of a word is usually spelled one of two ways:
- An -___ with a <u>silent</u> -___ on the end (as in *hope*).
- An -_____ (as in *coat*).

If the word *ends* with a **long -o** sound, it is usually spelled with an -____ (as in *snow*).
Occasionally it is spelled with an -___ (as in *go* and *no*) or an -_____ (as in *toe*).

Complete the clues with words that end with the **long -o** sound.

blow	crow	foe
go	grow	no
row	slow	snow
throw	toes	woe

1. What winds do; what you do to a trumpet: _____.

2. You have ten of these on the ends of your feet: _____.

3. Green light: _____.

4. What you do to a boat: _____.

5. What you need in order to have a white Christmas: _____.

6. Process by which we get taller: _____.

7. Trouble, misery, personal disaster: _____.

8. A black bird known for stealing: _____.

9. Opposite of yes: _____.

10. Opposite of fast: _____.

11. An enemy: _____.

12. To toss or pitch: _____.

Day 126

> **Clue:** The **long -o** sound in the *middle* of a word is usually spelled one of two ways:
> - An **-___** with a <u>silent</u> **-___** on the end (as in *hope*).
> - An **-_____** (as in *coat*).
>
> If the word **ends** with a **long -o** sound, it is usually spelled with an **-____** (as in *snow*).
> Occasionally it is spelled with an **-__** (as in *go* and *no*) or an **-_____** (as in *toe*).

Fill in the clues with words that end with the **long -o** sound.

bow	flow	glow
hoe	Joe	know
low	mow	show
so	sow	tow

1. Lightbulbs and lightning bugs do this: _____.

2. If you comprehend something, you _____ it.

3. A play or musical: _____.

4. What a river should do: _____.

5. Question: Because why?
   Answer: Because I said _____.

6. A girl likes to wear this in her hair: _____.

7. To plant a field: _____.

8. Not high: _____.

9. What you do to your grass when it gets too long: _____.

10. A boys name; short for Joseph: _____.

11. What you do to your garden to get rid of weeds: _____.

12. If your car breaks down you'll need a _____ truck.

Day 127

> **Clue:** The **long -o** sound in the *middle* of a word is usually spelled one of two ways:
> - An -___ with a **silent** -___ on the end (as in *hope*).
> - An -_____ (as in *coat*).
>
> If the word **ends** with a **long -o** sound, it is usually spelled with an -____ (as in *snow*).
> Occasionally it is spelled with an -___ (as in *go* and *no*) or an -_____ (as in *toe*).

Complete the Bible verses with **long -o** words.

boat	goats	hole
loaf	oak	robe
Rome	smoke	strove
	suppose	

1. "That is why I am so eager to preach the gospel also to you who are at _____." Romans 1:15

2. "The infant will play near the the _____ of the cobra..." Isaiah 11:8

3. "They clothed Him in a purple _____." John 19:2

4. "...As _____ to the eyes, so is a sluggard to those who send him." Proverbs 10:26

5. "These were the waters of Meribah, where the Israelites _____ with the LORD..." Numbers 20:13

6. "...He will separate the people one from another as a shepherd separates the sheep from the _____." Mat. 25:32

7. "The disciples had forgotten to bring bread except for one _____ they had with them in the _____." Mk. 8:14

8. "I just saw Absalom hanging in an _____ tree." 2 Sam. 18:10

9. "These men are not drunk, as you _____. It's only nine in the morning." Acts 2:15

Day 128

> **Clue:** The **long -o** sound in the *middle* of a word is usually spelled one of two ways:
> - An -___ with a <u>silent</u> -___ on the end (as in *hope*).
> - An -_____ (as in *coat*).
>
> If the word *ends* with a **long -o** sound, it is usually spelled with an -____ (as in *snow*).
> Occasionally it is spelled with an -___ (as in *go* and *no*) or an -_____ (as in *toe*).

Solve the clues with **long -o words** (the first letter is given), then find them in the puzzle (float, foam, froze, gloat, grove, Joan, joke, mole, oath, quo, roam, yoyo, zone).

1. Riddle, pun, or trick: j_____.
2. What a piece of styrofoam will do on water: f_____.
3. A round toy that winds up and down a string: y_____.
4. A small burrowing animal like a mouse: m_____.
5. Brag or boast over your victory and his defeat: g_____.
6. Rows of fruit trees; an orange g_____.
7. Status q_____.
8. A woman's name: J_____ of Arc.
9. A limited area: z_____.
10. Past tense of freeze: f_____.
11. The fizzy stuff on top of a glass of soda: f_____.
12. To wander around: r_____.
13. A covenant or promise: o_____.

t	q	o	a	t	h	w	e	r	e	n	o	z
a	t	y	u	y	i	i	o	p	a	s	u	d
o	f	g	j	o	k	e	h	t	j	k	q	l
l	z	x	c	y	v	l	a	b	j	o	a	n
f	o	a	m	o	n	o	m	f	r	o	z	e
q	w	e	r	t	l	m	y	u	i	k	p	a
e	v	o	r	g	s	d	f	g	r	o	a	m

Day 129

Clue: The **long -o** sound in the *middle* of a word is usually spelled one of two ways:
- An -___ with a **silent** -___ on the end (as in *hope*).
- An -_____ (as in *coat*).

If the word *ends* with a **long -o** sound, it is usually spelled with an -____ (as in *snow*).
Occasionally it is spelled with an -___ (as in *go* and *no*) or an -_____ (as in *toe*).

Solve the puzzle with the following **long -o** words: *choke, clove, home, note, photo, piano, potato, quote, remote, rowboat, stove, woke.*

Across
2. A picture taken with a camera.
3. A spice like cinnamon.
4. In music, "C" is one. So is "G."
6. The control that flips TV channels.
7. A keyboard instrument.
8. Past tense of wake.
9. Say it word-for-word.
10. What a French fry is made of.

Down
1. What you cook on.
3. When something is caught in your throat.
5. Where you live.
6. A small man-powered floating vessel.

Day 130 Review

Clue: The **long -o** sound in the *middle* of a word is usually spelled one of two ways:
- An -___ with a <u>silent</u> -___ on the end (as in *hope*).
- An -_____ (as in *coat*).

If the word **ends** with a **long -o** sound, it is usually spelled with an -____ (as in *snow*).
Occasionally it is spelled with an -__ (as in *go* and *no*) or an -_____ (as in *toe*).

Clue: Contractions are _____ words put together to form _____ word. An apostrophe is used to mark the _____ letters.
- In most contractions, the spelling of the first word _____ change.
- Instead, two words are _____ together and letters are_____ _____.
- An apostrophe is placed where the letters_____ ___ ___.
- The trick is to remember how to _____ the two words, don't _____ the spelling, and put an apostrophe where the letters_____ ___ ___.

Clue: When adding suffixes to words ending with y...
- When you are adding a suffix (ending) to a word that ends in _____, you should change the _____ to an _____, *then* add the_____.
- When adding a suffix (ending) to a word that ends in a vowel + y, do _____ change the _____ to an_____, or you'll have too many _____ in a row.
- When you are adding the suffix -ing to a word, do _____ change the _____ to an_____, or you'll have _____ i's in a_____.

Clue: When a word with two or more syllables _____ with the -ull sound, it is usually spelled with an _____.

Using the spelling clues above and the clues in parantheses below, complete the following sentences.

1. As the old saying goes, "_____(there + is) no place like _____ (hoam)." Some of your _____ (happy + est)_____ (memory + es) are formed with your family around the kitchen _____ (tabull).

2. _____ (Is + not) it true that our _____ (family + es) are _____(suppoasd) to be _____ (exampulls) of God's dealings with us. _____(We + are) His children and _____ (He + is) our Father.

3. God is _____ (abull) and can help _____ (thoas) _____ (family +es) who are in need of His grace. When we _____ (are + not) _____ (abull), He is _____ (abull).

Day 131

> **Clue:** The following words are common but don't follow the spelling rules:
> - The word *said* is the past tense of *say*. Both words begin with an **-sa**.
> - The word *are* is pronounced as if it didn't have an **-e** on the end.
> - The word *again* is also spelled as if it has a **long -a**. Pronouncing the word the way they do in England (with a long -a) will help you remember its spelling.

Complete the following sentences with *said, are,* or *again*.

1. How _____ you?

2. He _____, " It's me _____."

3. Could you please explain it _____?

4. _____ you going to the services tonight?

5. We _____ definitely interested.

6. Carolyn _____ she'd babysit.

7. God _____, "Let there be light!"

8. Come _____!

9. You _____ too short to ride this ride.

10. I heard what you _____.

11. How can you stand going through all that _____?

12. When we _____ weak, He is strong.

13. I couldn't hear what he _____.

Day 132

> **Clue:** The following words are common but don't follow the spelling rules:
> - The word _____ is the past tense of *say*. Both words begin with an -____.
> - The word *are* is pronounced as if it didn't have an -___ on the end.
> - The word *again* is also spelled as if it has a **long** -___. Pronouncing the word the way they do in England (with a long -a) will help you remember its spelling.

Complete the Bible verses with the words *said*, *are*, or *again*.

1. "_____ you've heard that it was _____ to the people long ago, 'Do not break your oath.'" Matthew 5:33

2. "You _____ a chosen generation." 1 Peter 2:9

3. "Unless a man is born _____, he cannot see the kingdom of God." John 3:3

4. "Blessed _____ those who _____ persecuted because of righteousness." Matthew 5:10

5. "You _____ the light of the world." Matthew 5:14

6. "But he _____ to them, 'It is I; don't be afraid.'" Jn. 6:20

7. "Rejoice in the Lord always, and _____ I say, Rejoice." Philippians 4:4

8. "He _____ unto the sea, 'Peace, be still.'" Mark 4:39

9. "You _____ the salt of the earth." Matthew 5:13

Day 133

Clue: The following words are common but don't follow the spelling rules:
- The word _____ is the past tense of *say*. Both words begin with an -____.
- The word **are** is pronounced as if it didn't have an -___ on the end.
- The word **again** is also spelled as if it has a **long** -___. Pronouncing the word the way they do in England (with a long -a) will help you remember its spelling.

Complete the Bible verses with the words *said, are,* or *again*.

1. "...Do good, and lend, hoping for nothing _____; and your reward shall be great." Luke 6:35

2. "He _____ to them, 'Make every effort to enter through the narrow door...'" Luke 13:23-24

3. "For you have been born _____, not of perishable seed, but of imperishable." 1 Peter 1:23

4. "Lord, _____ you going to wash my feet?" John 13:6

5. "If you _____ the Christ, tell us plainly." John 10:24

6. "Jesus _____, 'Feed my lambs.'" John 21:15

7. "I and the Father _____ one." John 10:30

8. "Women received back their dead raised to life _____." Hebrews 1:35

9. "Jesus _____, 'It is finished.'" John 19:30

Day 134

> **Clue:** The following words are common but don't follow the spelling rules:
> - The word _____ is the past tense of *say*. Both words begin with an -____.
> - The word **_are_** is pronounced as if it didn't have an -____ on the end.
> - The word **_again_** is also spelled as if it has a **long -____**. Pronouncing the word the way they do in England (with a long -a) will help you remember its spelling.

Fill in the blanks with the words *are, said,* and *again.*

1. Who _____ they wanted something to drink?

2. We need to be born _____.

3. Where _____ you going?

4. I _____ I wasn't ready.

5. She _____ she would do it.

6. I can't believe it's snowing _____.

7. Do you need dental xrays _____?

8. _____ we having company?

9. Where _____ the Bergens?

10. Stephen _____ that his foot hurt.

11. I have no idea where those wires _____.

12. We _____ going camping in Virginia _____.

Day 135

Clue: The following words are common but don't follow the spelling rules:
- The word _____ is the past tense of *say*. Both words begin with an -____.
- The word *are* is pronounced as if it didn't have an -____ on the end.
- The word *again* is also spelled as if it has a **long** -____. Pronouncing the word the way they do in England (with a long -a) will help you remember its spelling.

Fill in the blanks with the words *are, again,* and *said.*

1. "I keep falling in love with Him over and over _____."

2. How _____ you?

3. Where _____ you from?

4. "Mom, look," Stephen _____.

5. Come _____.

6. "I do," the bride _____.

7. Where _____ your parents?

8. God _____, "I love you."

9. It's time to feed the baby _____.

10. Do you know where your children _____?

11. Could you check the cake _____, please?

12. Who _____ they wanted to go first?

Day 136

> **Clue:** The following words are common but don't follow the spelling rules:
> - **_Does_** is the verb *do* with an **-es** on the end.
> - **_From_** is spelled with an **-o**. When addressing an envelope, you write who the letter is *to* and who the letter is *from*.
> - **_Have_** sounds like a short –a, but is spelled like a long –a. Remember it this way: **H**a**ve** you been s**ave**d?
> - **_Can_** is pronounced *ken*. If you *can* spell *can't*, you *can* spell *can*.

Use the words *does, from, have,* and *can* to fill in the blanks.

1. How _____ your garden grow?

2. Do we _____ any bandaids left?

3. I _____ never remember his name.

4. Who is that package _____?

5. How _____ he do that?

6. I got that _____ Mexico.

7. You _____ do it!

8. I _____ three more pieces left.

9. Carlo _____ not want any more.

10. These are my friends _____ Tennessee.

Day 137

Clue: The following words are common but don't follow the spelling rules:
- _____ is the verb *do* with an -___ on the end.
- <u>*Fr m*</u> is spelled with an -___. When addressing an envelope, you write who the letter is ____ and who the letter is _____.
- <u>*Have*</u> sounds like it has a short -____, but is spelled like a long -_____. Remember it this way: H_____ you been s____d?
- _____ is pronounced *ken*. If you *can* spell _____, you *can* spell _____.

Complete the Bible passages with *does, from, have,* and *can.*

1. "How _____ a young man keep his way pure?" Psalm 119:9

2. "Where _____ my help come _____? My help comes _____ the LORD." Psalm 121:1-2

3. "You _____ commanded us to keep your precepts diligently." Psalm 119:4

4. "With my whole heart I _____ sought you." Psalm 119:10

5. "Remove _____ me reproach and contempt." Psalm 119:22

6. "Whatever the LORD pleases He _____." Psalm 135:6

7. "Where _____ I go _____ Your Spirit? Or where _____ I flee _____ Your presence?" Psalm 139:7

8. "Remove _____ me the way of lying." Psalm 119:29

Day 138

> **Clue:** The following words are common but don't follow the spelling rules:
> - _____ is the verb *do* with an -___ on the end.
> - *Fr_m* is spelled with an -__. When addressing an envelope, you write who the letter is ____ and who the letter is _____.
> - *Have* sounds like it has a short -____, but is spelled like a long -_____. Remember it this way: H_____ you been s____d?
> - _____ is pronounced *ken*. If you *can* spell _____, you *can* spell _____.

Complete these sentences with *does, from, have,* and *can*.

1. _____ anyone _____ a pencil I _____ borrow for this test?

2. We just got a package _____ Grandmom.

3. The new family _____ Kansas _____ use some help moving all those boxes.

4. Helena _____ not want any help _____ the boys.

5. She _____ do it herself.

6. _____ you _____ Jeff take out the trash?

7. Isaac really _____ _____ a lot of talent!

8. We just found out that Troy _____ _____ that old table _____ Grandpa Miller.

9. How _____ we make sure this package _____ the church arrives on the mission field on time?

Day 139

Clue: The following words are common but don't follow the spelling rules:
- _____ is the verb *do* with an -____ on the end.
- *Fr_m* is spelled with an -__. When addressing an envelope, you write who the letter is ____ and who the letter is _____.
- *Have* sounds like it has a short -____, but is spelled like a long -_____. Remember it this way: H_____ you been s____d?
- _____ is pronounced *ken*. If you *can* spell _____, you *can* spell _____.

Use *does, from, have,* and *can* to complete the Bible verses below.

1. "My frame was not hidden _____ You when I was made in secret…" Psalm 139:15

2. "They _____ spread a net by the wayside; they _____ set traps for me." Psalm 140:5

3. "Keep me _____ the snares they _____ laid for me." Psalm 141:9

4. "If the foundations are destroyed, what _____ the righteous do?" Psalm 11:3

5. "There is none who _____ good, no, not one." Psalm 14:3

6. "For by You I _____ run against a troop, by my God I _____ leap over a wall." Psalm 18:29

7. "Deliver me, O LORD, _____ evil men; preserve me _____ violent men…" Psalm 140:1

8. "Lord, who may abide in Your tabernacle?…He who _____ not backbite with his tongue, nor _____ evil to his neighbor, nor _____ he take up a reproach against his friend…." Psalm 15:1, 3

Day 140 Review

Clue: The following words are common but don't follow the spelling rules:
- The word _____ is the past tense of *say*. Both words begin with an -____.
- The word **are** is pronounced as if it didn't have an -____ on the end.
- The word **again** is also spelled as if it has a **long** -____. Pronouncing the word the way they do in England (with a long –a) will help you remember its spelling.

Clue: The following words are common but don't follow the spelling rules:
- _____ is the verb *do* with an -____ on the end.
- **Fr_m** is spelled with an -____. When addressing an envelope, you write who the letter is ____ and who the letter is _____.
- **Have** sounds like it has a short -____, but is spelled like a long -____. Remember it this way: H_____ you been s____d?
- _____ is pronounced **ken**. If you *can* spell _____, you *can* spell _____.

Clue: The words "because" and "before" both begin with a _____ and end with a silent _____.
- _____ has an –aw- sound that is spelled with an –_____-.
- _____ has the word "_____" in the middle

The words "always" and "almost" both begin with an _____-.
- _____ ends with the word "_____."
- _____ ends with the word "_____."

Clue: If a *short-vowel* word or syllable ends with a –j sound, the –j sound is usually spelled with a -_____.

Complete the sentences below using the spelling clues above and the clues in parentheses in the following sentences.

1. We _____ (ar) making _____ (fuj) _____(becuz) we _____ (ken) give it to Grandpop for his Birthday. It is _____ (all + most) time to go. We need to get there _____ (be4) he _____ (duz)!

2. He _____ (all _ways) sleeps right on the _____ (ej) of his bed. He might fall _____ (agen) if he _____ (duz) not learn to sleep further _____ (frum) the _____ (ej).

3. You _____ (ken) _____ (hav) this _____(baj).

Day 141

Clue: The **long -e** sound is *usually* spelled one of two ways:
- With an **-ea** as in cl**ea**n,
- With an **-ee** as in tr**ee**.

In the chart below fill in the **-ea** in each of the long -e words.

b___ns	bl___ch	cl___n	f___r
h___t	m___l	m___n	s___t
t___ch	t___m	wh___t	y___r

Using the words from the chart above, complete the sentences below with long -e words.

1. I don't know what you _____ by that.

2. My _____ was in the second row.

3. The 90 degree _____ was oppressive.

4. Some people have a _____ of heights.

5. Our garden produced several bushels of green _____.

6. Could you please _____ up the kitchen when you're done?

7. Mary is going to _____ me how to knit.

8. I prefer whole _____ bread.

9. The Phillies are our local baseball _____.

10. Michael got his license one _____ ago.

11. For breakfast we had oat _____.

12. I needed to _____ the socks to remove the stains.

Day 142

Clue: The **long -e** sound is *usually* spelled one of two ways:
- With an -_____ as in cl**ea**n,
- With an -_____ as in tr**ee**.

In the chart below fill in the **-ee** in each of the long –e words.

f___d	f___t	gr___dy	k___p
m___k	n___d	s___k	sh___p
sl___p	sw___t	tr___s	w___p

Complete the following verses with –ee words from the chart above.

1. "_____ first the kingdom of God and His righteousness." Mt. 6:33

2. "And all the _____ of the field shall clap their hands." Isaiah 55:12

3. "Deacons must be reverent…not _____ for money." 1 Tim. 3:8

4. "My God shall supply all you _____ according to His riches in glory by Christ Jesus." Philippians 4:19

5. "Now it is high time to awake out of _____." Romans 13:11

6. "You will _____ him in perfect peace whose mind is stayed on You….." Isaiah 26:3

7. "_____ my _____." John 21:17

8. "To everything there is a season…a time to _____ and a time to laugh." Ecclesiastes 3:4

9. "Having shod your _____ with the preparation of the gospel of peace." Ephesians 6:15

10. "May my meditation be _____ to Him." Psalm 104:34

11. "For I am _____ and lowly in heart." Matthew 11:29

Day 143

Clue: The **long -e** sound is *usually* spelled one of two ways:
- With an -_____ as in cl**ea**n,
- With an -_____ as in tr**ee**.

Use one pair of homophones from the chart below in each sentence.

beat - to hit; to go faster than	**beet** – a vegetable
dear - opening for a letter	**deer** - an animal
flea - an insect	**flee** - to run away
heel – part of your foot	**heal** - to get better
meat – animal flesh	**meet** – to become acquainted with
peek - a quick look	**peak** – the top of a mountain
read - to decipher writing	**reed** - a water plant
see - to look	**sea** - a body of water
seem - to appear as if	**seam** - where cloth is sewed together
team - a group of players	**teem** - to mob
week - seven days	**weak** - not strong

1. My _____ had a sore that wouldn't _____.

2. _____ Tony, We saw three _____ in our campsite today.

3. After fasting for a _____, Pastor Glen felt physically _____.

4. The award-winning _____ from our garden was so large that it _____ the previous record.

5. I'd like to _____ the story of baby Moses in the _____ basket.

6. When our _____ wins, the stadium will _____ with fans.

7. When I saw that _____ on the dog, I wanted to _____.

8. I couldn't wait to _____ the Mediterranean _____.

9. I would like to _____ the chef who cooked the delicious _____.

10. I took a _____ to see if clouds covered the mountain _____.

11. It would _____ like you tore the _____ of your pants.

Day 144

Clue: The **long -e** sound is *usually* spelled one of two ways:
- With an -_____ as in cl**ea**n,
- With an -_____ as in tr**ee**.

In the chart below fill in the **-ee** in each of the long –e words, then use the words from the chart to complete the sentences.

b__s	b__f	ch__r	cr__p
f__l	fr__	kn__	qu__n
scr__n	str__t	thr__	w__ds

1. These insects make honey: _____.

2. When you don't have to pay for something, it is _____.

3. What you do when your team wins: _____.

4. What a baby will do before it will learn to crawl: _____.

5. What you have growing, unwelcome, in your garden: _____.

6. A road or lane: _____.

7. Meat from a cow: _____.

8. The sense centered in your fingertips: _____.

9. One, two, _____, four, five…

10. A leg joint: _____.

11. Married to the king: _____.

12. A TV and a computer has this: _____.

Day 145

Clue: The **long -e** sound is *usually* spelled one of two ways:
- With an -_____ as in cl**ea**n,
- With an -_____ as in tr**ee**.

In the chart below fill in the **-ea** in each of the long –e words, then use those words to complete the Bible verses. Some words are used twice.

cl__n__	__ch	f__r	f__st
h__l	h__r	l__p	n__r
pr__ch	r__p	w__k	

1. "For when I am _____, then I am strong." 2 Cor. 12:10

2. "For whatever a man sows, that he will also _____." Gal. 5:7

3. If anyone has ears to _____, let him _____!" Mk. 7:16

4. "Let _____ esteem others better than himself." Phil. 2:3

5. "Go into all the world and _____ the gospel to every creature." Mark 16:15

6. "He who is of a merry heart has a continual _____."Prov.15:15

7. "Rejoice in that day and _____ for joy!" Luke 6:23

8. "If You are willing, You can make me _____."Mark 1:40

9. "He gave them power...to _____ all kinds of sickness." Mat. 10:1

10. "There is no _____ in love; but perfect love casts out _____." 1 John 4:18

11. "Draw _____ to God and He will draw _____ to you." James 4:8

Day 146

Clue: The **long -e** sound is *usually* spelled one of two ways:
- With an -_____ as in cl**ea**n,
- With an -_____ as in tr**ee**.

Complete the puzzle below with long –e words. Use these words: *cheek, clean, cream, creed, east, gear, heat, lean, neat, real, seed, streak, stream, treat, wheel, year.*

Across
3. A piece of candy is a _____.
4. A car with manual transmission will have first, second, and third _____.
6. May is a month; 2001 is a _____.
7. Ice _____ cone.
9. If you were weak, you would _____ on someone for support.
11. Jesus said to turn the other _____.
12. North, south, _____, west.
14. To boil water, turn up the _____.
15. Washing hands makes them _____.

Down
1. A small river or creek.
2. A flash or _____ of lightning.
5. Not fake.
7. Both Catholic and Protestant churches recite the Apostle's __.
8. A tire is mounted on a _____.
10. When everything is put away, the house is _____.
13. Plants grow from a _____.

Day 147

Clue: The **long -e** sound is *usually* spelled one of two ways:
- With an -_____ as in cl**ea**n,
- With an -_____ as in tr**ee**.

Complete the sentences with long –e words from the chart.

beads	green	greet	leaf
peach	sheets	steam	steer
sweep	tea	teen	veal

1. Robert Fulton invented the _____ boat.

2. To keep a car on the road, you must _____ it.

3. A person between the ages of twelve and twenty is a _____ ager.

4. A bed should have fresh _____.

5. During the holidays we _____ each other with, "Merry Christmas!"

6. To clean the kitchen floor, you _____ it.

7. When you mix blue and yellow, you get _____.

8. Meat from a young cow is called _____.

9. A hot drink is _____.

10. A part of a tree is a _____.

11. A necklace is made from _____.

12. A fruit with a fuzzy skin is a _____.

Day 148

> **Clue:** The **long -e** sound is *usually* spelled one of two ways:
> - With an -_____ as in cl**ea**n,
> - With an -_____ as in tr**ee**.

Complete the words in the chart, then use them in the sentences below.

ea		ee	
b__st	m__n__	b__-__	b__f
r__d	sp__k	d__p	qu__n
y__st	z__l	st__p	thr__-__

1. Disney made a cartoon called *Beauty and the* _____.

2. The godhead is made up of _____ persons: the Father, the Son and the Holy Spirit.

3. For bread to rise, it must have _____.

4. Meat from a cow is _____.

5. Excitement and enthusiasm is _____.

6. The sides of a mountain are _____.

7. Someone who isn't kind is _____.

8. The opposite of shallow is _____.

9. When spoken to, you should _____.

10. In a hive, all the work revolves around the _____ _____.

11. You should _____ the Bible daily.

Day 149

Clue: The **long -e** sound is *usually* spelled one of two ways:
- With an -_____ as in cl**ea**n,
- With an -_____ as in tr**ee**.

Fill in the blanks, then find the long –e words in the puzzle.

Q	W	E	R	T	Y	U	T	I	O	P	A
S	D	B	F	G	K	A	H	D	J	K	L
L	Z	E	X	C	E	D	E	E	R	V	A
T	E	A	R	H	E	R	B	E	N	M	E
Q	W	K	C	E	W	E	E	P	E	A	S
F	E	A	R	E	R	A	T	S	Y	U	I
O	P	B	A	S	D	M	F	G	H	J	K

1. A collie is one _____ of dog; a poodle is another.

2. When afraid, we feel _____.

3. A story in your head while you sleep is called a _____.

4. Another word for cry is _____.

5. A buck or a doe is a _____.

6. When driving, please obey the _____ limit.

7. Seven days equals one _____.

8. A vegetable we often eat for dinner is _____.

9. When you cry, this will come from your eye: _____.

10. A bird's mouth is called a _____.

11. An animal that can balance a ball on his nose and has flippers rather than feet is called a _____.

12. It is no fun to play games with people who _____.
    (Use these words: beak, breed, cheat, deer, dream, fear, peas, seal, speed, tear, week, weep)

Day 150

Clue: The **long -e** sound is *usually* spelled one of two ways:
- With an -_____ as in cl**ea**n,
- With an -_____ as in tr**ee**.

Clue: The **long -o** sound in the *middle* of a word is usually spelled one of two ways:
- An -___ with a **silent** -___ on the end (as in *hope*).
- An -_____ (as in *coat*).

If the word **ends** with a **long -o** sound, it is usually spelled with an -____ (as in *snow*).
Occasionally it is spelled with an -___ (as in *go* and *no*) or an -_____ (as in *toe*).

Clue: The **long -a** sound is usually spelled one of three ways. These spellings must be memorized:
- With an -_____ as in **train**.
- With an -___ followed by a **silent** -____ on the end, as in **save**.
- If the word *ends* with the long -a sound, it is usually spelled with an -____.

Clue: The following words are common but don't follow the spelling rules:
- _____ is the verb *do* with an -___ on the end.
- **Fr _ m** is spelled with an -___. When addressing an envelope, you write who the letter is ____and who the letter is_____.
- **Have** sounds like it has a short -_____, but is spelled like a long -____. Remember it this way: H_____ you been s____d?
- _____is pronounced **ken**. If you **can** spell _____, you **can** spell _____.

Using the spelling clues above and the clues in the parentheses, complete the following sentences.

1. We _____ (caim) _____ (hoam) by _____(trane) _____ (frum) the _____(Eest) _____ (coste).

2. _____ (Duz) he _____ (hav) the assignment _____(frum) the _____(teecher) for this _____(weak's) lessons?

3. Our _____ (hoap) is in Jesus, and our _____ (fathe) is in Jesus. He is the One who _____ (saivs) us _____(frum) our sin. He _____(sed) we are _____(cleen) before Him because of His gift of _____ (graic).

Notes Concerning Exceptions   (Page 151)

Lessons 25-29 (Ending -ch sound is spelled with a -tch...)

There are several common words that are exceptions to this rule, such as *which, much, and such.* *Teach, preach,* and *reach* have long vowel sounds, so they end only in -ch. Also, if a word ends with another consonant plus the -ch sound, then you don't use the silent -t (like -rch as in *porch, perch,* and *torch* OR -nch as in *lunch, bench,* and *pinch*).

Lessons 35-39 (Contractions...)

Most contractions follow the rules. The exception is the common contraction for *will + not.* It is spelled *won't.*

Lessons 51-54 (Ending syllable spelled with an -le...)

There are several common words that don't follow this rule but end in an -el, including *panel, funnel, tunnel, model,* and *camel.* Occasionally a word may end in -al, as in *medal, metal, pedal, petal, fatal,* and *personal.* Rarely, a word will end in -ol (*carol*) or -ul (*annul*).

Lessons 55-59 (I before e except after c...)

The trick here is to realize there are several other ways to spell the long -e sound besides -ie. These are reviewed in lessons 141-149. One exception to the *i before e* rule is the word *height* which has the long -i sound, but is spelled with an -ei. Another exception is *leisure.*

Lessons 61-69 (Ending syllable spelled -tion...)

There are a number of common words that end in -sion, such as *mission, passion, permission,* and *confusion.* A few words end in -cian such as *physician, magician,* and *musician.* Notice that the root of each of these three words end in the letter -c (*physic, magic, music*).

Lesson 71-74 (Long -i spelled -ight...)

Some words with a long -i sound are spelled with an -ite, such as *bite, kite, quite,* and *white.*

Lessons 85-89 (Ending syllable spelled -ture...)

There are a few *root* words that end in -ch or -tch that add the *suffix* -er, such as *teacher, preacher,* and *pitcher.* In these cases, the -cher sound at the end is not spelled with a -ture. Just remember these words have a root that **can stand alone** (*teach, preach, pitch*).

Lessons 95-99 (Ending -j sound spelled as -dge in short-vowel words ...)
There are several words that end with a -j sound but are spelled with a -ge rather than a -dge. These words have long-vowel sounds rather than short vowel sounds (*cage, rage, sage*).

Lessons 101-104 (The -or sound...)
The hardest part of this lesson is to remember that many -or words need a silent -e on the end (*store, more, adore*) unless the word ends in a consonant other than -r (*storm, corn, fort*). There are only a few words that do not end with either another consonant or a silent -e (*nor, for, or*).

Lessons 111-119 (Long -a...)
There are at least two other ways to spell the long -a sound, but they are not used often. They are:
- -ey (as in *obey* and *they*)
- -ei (as in *weigh, their,* and *eight*)

Lessons 121-129 (Long -o...)
There are at least four other ways to spell the long -o sound, but they are not used often. They are:
- -ow (as in *know, snow,* and *own*)
- -oe (as in *toe* and *Joe*)
- -old (as in *sold, gold,* and *told*)
- -ost (as in *host, most,* and *post*)

Lessons 141-149 (Long -e...)
There are several other ways to spell the long -e. The first two are not used often. They are:
- -e+consonant+silent -e (as in *these, scene,* and *here*)
- -ey (as in *key, money,* and *donkey*)
- -ie (as in *field, thief,* and *belief*)

Also, a number of long -e words also *end* in a silent -e. Study these examples: *believe, cheese, sleeve, please, peace, leave.*

Answer Key (page 153)

Day 1: Patted, patting, clapped, clapping, skipped, skipping, hopped, hopping; 1. Slipping, 2. patted, 3. clapped, 4. hopping, 5. skipped; Pinning, singing, eating, hanging, clipping, slapping, parting, shipping, shopping, snapping, keeping, trimming.

Day 2: Clue: suffix, consonant, short, double; 1. Grabbed, grabbing, mopped, mopping, budded, budding, wedded, wedding; 2. Slipped, clapped, grabbed, hopping, slapped, slipped, begging, slopping, begged, hugged.

Day 3: Clue: suffix, consonant, short, double; 1. Clubbed, clubbing, rubbed, rubbing, pitted, pitting, trimmed, trimming, slammed, slamming; 2. (going down) B, A, A, A, A, A, B, A, B, B, B, A.

Day 4: Clue: suffix, consonant, short, double; 1.compelling, forgetting, kidnapping, combatting, abetting, hobnobbing, upsetting, babysitting, expelling, abutting, committing, humbugging; 2. . Rammed, licked, potted, pushed, chilled, padded, dipped, lumped, chipped, chatted, camped, mocked, skinned, chopped, bobbed.

Day 5: Clue: suffix, consonant, short, double; Circle the following: 1. claping (A - clapping), wavving (C - waving), 2. Diging (A - digging), poting (A - potting), 3. Choped (A - chopped), campping (B - camping), 4. Forgeting (A - forgetting), strivving (C - striving), 5. Skined (A - skinned), chiped (A - chipped); . Chugged, chugging, shipped, shipping, dabbed, dabbing, hummed, humming.

Day 6: About, alone, allow, another, aloof, again, around, aloud, along, amaze; 1. Aloof, 2. another, 3. about, 4. around, 5. alone, 6. aloud, 7. allow, 8. along, 9. again, again, 10. amaze; 11. About, another, 12. amazing, around, 13. along, alone, 14. allow, again

Day 7: Clue: the "uh" sound, "a"; Abandon, again, about, abide, abuse, ability, above, abound, abolish, across; 1. Abound, 2. abuse, 3. across, 4. abandon, 5. again, 6. abolish, 7. about, 8. above, 9. abide, 10. ability; . Umbrella-B, again-A, around-A, umpire-B, about-A, upsetting-B, ugly-B, amaze-A.

Day 8: Clue: the "uh" sound, "a"; 1. ashore, 2. ahead, 3. afraid, 4. away, 5. amount, 6. against, 7. alarm, 8. apart, 9. agree, 10. adapt, 11. apology, 12. alive, 13. Alaska, 14. amuse, 15. aroma, 16. adopted.

Day 9: Clue: the "uh" sound, "a"; Astonish-A, atomic-A, uncle-B, uproar-B, awake-A, underneath-B, awhile-A, aware-A, astray-A, award-A; 1. About, awake, 2. afraid, alive, 3. aware, astonished, 4. awhile, away, 5. apology, again, 6. Alaska, adapt, 7.astray, adopt.

Day 10 Review: Clue: suffix, ends with a single consonant, has a short vowel sound, double; Clue: the "uh" sound, "a"; 1. Alaska, 2. away, 3. winning, 4. spitting, 5. bidding, 6. again, 7. batting, 8. another, 9. against, 10. begging.

Day 11: 1. o, 2. ue, 3. e, 4. ur, 5. r, 6. il, 7. y, 8. u, 9. c, 10. day, 11. ary, 12. Au, 13. capital.

Day 12: Clue: Sunday, Monday, Tuesday, Wednesday, Thursday, Friday, Saturday, day, January, February, March, April, May, June, July, August, September, October, November, December, ber, capitalize 1. Sunday, 2. Wednesday, 3. July, 4. December, 5. March, April, Sunday, 6. November, Thursday, 7. February,8. Saturday, Sunday, 9. Monday, 10. August, September, 11. Tuesday.

Day 13: Clue: Sunday, Monday, Tuesday, Wednesday, Thursday, Friday, Saturday, day, January, February, March, April, May, June, July, August, September, October, November, December, ber, capitalize. 1. Saturday, 2. May, 3. June, 4. October, 5. Friday, 6. Tuesday, 7. January, 8. Wednesday,9. Tuesday, 10. Thursday, 11. February, 12. December, 13. August.

(Page 154)

Day 14: Clue: Sunday, Monday, Tuesday, Wednesday, Thursday, Friday, Saturday, day, January, February, March, April, May, June, July, August, September, October, November, December, ber, capitalize. 1. July 4, 1776; 2. January 1, 2000; 3. February 22, 1732; 4. teacher check; 5. July 19, 1969; 6. April 4, 1968; 7. December 7, 1941; 8. October 24, 1929; 9. June 6, 1944; 10. August 15, 1945.

Day 15: Clue: Sunday, Monday, Tuesday, Wednesday, Thursday, Friday, Saturday, day, January, February, March, April, May, June, July, August, September, October, November, December, ber, capitalize. 1. Saturday, 2. Tuesday, Thursday, 3. March, June, 4. September, 5. December, 6. February, 7. August, 8. January, February, March, 9. April, May, June, 10. July, September, October, 11. November, December.

Day 16: Sentences 4 and 11 use the word "you're," while the rest of the sentences use the word "your."

Day 17: Clue: you're, you are, a, you are, you're, your, possession, r; sentences 5 and 12 use the word "your," while the rest of the sentences use the word "you're."

Day 18: Clue: you're, you are, a, you are, you're, your, possession, r; 1. you're, 2. you're, 3. your, 4. you're, 5. you're, 6. your, 7. you're, 8. your, 9. you're, your, 10. your, 11. your, you're, 12. you're.

Day 19: Clue: you're, you are, a, you are, you're, your, possession, r; 1. you're, your, your, your; 2. you're, your, your; 3. your; 4. you're, your, your; 5. your; 6. you're; 7. you're; 8. you're, your; 9. you're, your.

Day 20: Clue: Monday, Tuesday, Wednesday, Thursday, Friday, Saturday, Sunday; day; January, February, March, April, May, June, July, August, September, October, November, December; ber, capitalize. Clue: you're, you are, a, you are, you're, your, possession, r; Clue: suffix, ends with a single consonant, has a short vowel sound, double; 1. Your, teacher correct, you're, planning; 2. You're, getting, your; 3. you're, you're, Thursday; 4. begging; 5. shopping.

Day 21: 1. When; 2. Where; 3. when; 4. where; 5. when, where; 6. When; 1. went; 2. Were; 3. were; 4. went; 5. went; 6. were; 7. went, were.

Day 22: Clue: When, h; Went, go, no; Were, be, we, were; Where, "here," here, where. 1. When, were; 2. where; 3. went, were; 4. were, went; 5. were, when; 6. were, went; 7. where, were; 8. when; 9. when.

Day 23: Clue: When, h; Went, go, no; Were, be, we, were; Where, "here," here, where. 1. When, went, 2. were, 3. were, where, 4. Where, 5. when, 6. Where, 7. were, when, 8. were, were, 9. were, 10. went, 11. were, were.

Day 24: Clue: When, h; Went, go, no; Were, be, we, were; Where, "here," here, where. 1. When, were; 2. were; 3. were; 4. when went; 5. where, were, when; 6. went; 7. were; 8. were; 9. when, when, when.

Day 25: 1. pitch, 2. match, 3. catch, 4. witch, 5. crutch, 6. watch, 7. batch, 8. fetch, 9. scratch, 10. Dutch, 11. ditch, 12. patch.

Day 26: Clue: tch; 1. bench, 2. watch, 3. fetch, 4. finch, 5. crutch, 6. botch, 7. much, 8. match, 9. wretch, 10. hitch, 11. bunch, 12. pinched, 13. catch, 14. which, witch, which.

Day 27: Clue: tch; 1. lunch, patch, much batch; 2. hatch, watch, Mitch, fetch; 3. watch, pitch, catch, such; 4. unhitch, pinched, match, botch.

Day 28: Clue: tch,. 1. Stretch, 2. Catch, 3. Crutch, 4. Clutch, 5. Patch, 6. Stitch, 7. Scratch, 8. Dutch, 9. Pitch, 10. Match, 11. Hitch, 12. Hutch.

Day 29: Clue: tch; 1. torch, porch, church, birch; 2. hunch, pinch, lunch, stretch; 3. watch, clutch, lurch, flinch; 4. crunch, latch, munch, scratch.

(Page 155)

Day 30 Review: Clue: When, h; Went, go, no; Were, be, we, were; Where, "here," here, where. Clue: tch; Clue: -a. 1. Away, 2. Adore, 3. When, 4. Where, where, were; 5. Watch, 6. Catchy 7. Adore.

Day 31: 1. To, two, to, 2. Too, to, 3. Two, to, too, 4. To, two, 5. Too, to, to, 6. Two, to, 7. Two, too, to, 8. To, to, 9. To, too, 10. To, to, 11. To, to, 12. To.

Day 32: Clue: two, 2, two, wheels, on, too, extremely, also, two, to most frequently, short; 1. Too, 2. To, 3. To, to, 4. To, 5. To, to, 6. To, 7. Too, 8. Two, to.

Day 33: Clue: two, 2, two, wheels, on, too, extremely, also, two, to most frequently, short; 1. To, 2. To, 3. To, too, 4. To, 5. To, too, 6. Two, to, 7, to, 8. To, 9. To, two, to, 10. To, to.

Day 34: Clue: two, 2, two, wheels, on, too, extremely, also, two, to most frequently, short; 1. To, 2. Two, 3. To, two, 4. Too. 5. Two, to, 6. To, 7. To, to, 8. To, too, 9. To, to, to, 10. To.

Day 35: Missing letters (going down the list): o,o, wi, i, a, wi, a, woul, woul, o, ha, a, ha, o, wi, a; 1. Don't, you're, 2. you'll, 3. could've, 4. wouldn't, 5. they'll, 6. that's, you'd, 7. she'd.

Day 36: Clue: two, one, missing, doesn't, squeezed, left out, used to be, spell, change, used to be; (going down the list) can not, you are, has, not, were not, it is, we are, he will, she is, should not, had not, could have, they are, you will, are not. 1. Didn't, 2. Don't, isn't, he'll, 3. He's, 4. We're, 5. I'm, 6. I've.

Day 37: Clue: two, one, missing, doesn't, squeezed, left out, used to be, spell, change, used to be; (going down) I'm, I'll, who's, that'll, wouldn't, isn't, they're, weren't, you're, we've, you've, we're, can't, who'll, she's, should've; 1. Should've, 2. he'll, 3.wasn't, 4.weren't, 5.didn't, couldn't, 6. you'll, you're.

Day 38: Clue: two, one, missing, doesn't, squeezed, left out, used to be, spell, change, used to be; (going down the list) Doesn't – o, we've – ha, they've – ha, I'd – woul, he's –i, we'll – wi, hasn't – o, who's – i, can't – no, weren't – o, we're – a, they'd – woul, I'm – a, who'll – wi, they're – a, those'll – wi; 1. There's, 2. nothing's, 3. I'll, 4. it's, 5. he'll, 6. it's, 7. we've.

Day 39: Clue: two, one, missing, doesn't, squeezed, left out, used to be, spell, change, used to be; (going down the list) aren't – o, shouldn't – o, she's – i, who'll – wi, we'll – wi, they're – a, we'd – woul, haven't – o, hasn't – o, it's – i, they'll – wi, we're – a, I'd – woul, you're – a; 1. Wouldn't, 2. you're, 3. we've, 4. aren't, 5. they're, 6. isn't, 7. don't, it's.

Day 40 – Review: clue 1 – two, 2, two, wheels, on, too, extreme, also, two, to, most, frequently, short; clue 2 – two one, missing, doesn't, squeezed, left out, used to be, spell, change, used to be; clue 3 – Sunday, Monday, Tuesday, Wednesday, Thursday, Friday, Saturday, day, January, February, March, April, May, June, July, August, September, October, November, December, ber, capitalize; 1. To, two, 2. too, 3. I'll, 4. who's, 5. I'll, 6. Tuesday, 7. Wednesday.

Day 41: 1. Rule – y, i , ed; babied married, hurried, worried, fried, accompanied, sanctified, prettied, carried, buried, tarried, cried, spied, occupied, justified, dirtied; Rule - y, i , er; merrier, carrier, heavier, stinkier, lovelier, fluffier, friendlier, runnier, happier, sloppier, prettier, uglier, dirtier, stubbier; Rule – y, i, es; babies, spies, families, puppies, pennies, lobbies, companies, enemies, cries, ladies, parties, mommies, hippies, cabbies, industries, cities.

Day 42: Clue: y, y, i, suffix; 1. Rule - y, i, est; merriest, grouchiest, heaviest, stinkiest, loveliest, fluffiest, friendliest, funniest, runniest, happiest, sloppiest, prettiest, ugliest, dirtiest, stubbiest, dizziest; 2. Rule – y, i, es; candies, cherries, ponies, bellies, buggies, pities, strawberries, flies, pansies, stories, replies, satisfies; 3. Ladies, babies; 4. Accompanied, mommies, daisies; 5. Bunnies, ponies.

(Page 156)

Day 43: Clue: y, y, i, suffix; 1. Worried, 2. Happiest, ladies; 3. Dirtier, stinkier, loveliest; 4. Justified, cried; 5. Hurried, babied; 6. Prettied, lovelier; 7. Merriest, families, accompanied; 8. Occupied, spied; 9. Satisfied, pennies; 10. Fried.

Day 44: 1. Rule – change y, vowels; played, employed, sprayed, monkeyed, honeyed, prayed, obeyed, frayed, grayed, strayed, moneyed, toyed, replayed, enjoyed; 2. Rule – change y, vowels; player, grayer, displayer, sprayer, buyer repayer; 3. Rule – change, y; plays, bays, sprays, monkeys, honeys, prays, replays, enjoys, displays, frays, grays, strays, donkeys, toys, pays, obeys, moneys, repays.

Day 45: Clue: y, y, i, ending, not, y, i, vowels; 1. (going across the list) enjoys, enjoyed, sprays, sprayed, sprayer, obeys, obeyed, plays, played, player, employs, employed, employer, buys, buyer; 2. (going down) joys, toys, chimneys, valleys, guys, ploys, boys, days, keys, donkeys, rays, trolleys; 3. Monkeyed, played, frayed; 4. Prayed, honeyed, obeyed, enjoyed, toyed.

Day 46: Clue: y, y, i, ending, not, y, i, vowels; 1. Moneyed, buys, pays, employed, 2. Monkeys, displayed, enjoyed, toys; 3. Employer, grayed, days, frayed; 4. Trollies, valleys, holidays; 5. Boys, enjoyed, birthdays, displayed; 6. Obeyed, says, prayed; 7. Guys, employed, grayer, sprayer; 8. Chimneys, grayed, rays.

Day 47: 1. (going down the list) playing, spraying, obeying, straying, replaying, displaying, copying, justifying, hurrying, marrying, accompanying, paying, praying, fraying, toying, enjoying, graying, trying, crying, carrying, flying, ferrying; 2. Y, i, not, y, i, vowels, not, y, i, i; 3. Justifying, sanctifying, enjoys, praying, obeying.

Day 48: Clue: y, y, i, suffix, not, y, i, vowels, not, y, i, i, row; 1. Babying; 2. Enjoying, crying; 3. Obeying, displaying; 4. Trying, copying; 5. Trying, carrying; 6. Disobeying, repaying; 7. Fraying, graying; 8. Praying, playing, enjoying.

Day 49: Clue: y, y, i, suffix, not, y, i, vowels, not, y, i, i, row; Y, i, not, y, i, vowels, not, y, i, i; 1. A – families, 2. b – Sundays, b – boys, b – Saturdays, 3. a – happiest, c – enjoying, 4. c – carrying, c – playing, c – praying, c – crying.

Day 50: Clue: when, h, went, go, no, were, be, we, were, where, here, her, where; Clue: two 2, two, wheels, on, too, extreme, also, two, to, most frequently, short; Clue: y, y, i, suffix, not, y, i, vowels, not, y, i, too many, row; 1. When, happier, your; 2. To, where, your, to; 3. Where, were, when; 4. When, went, to, sorrier.

Day 51: (going down the lists) bottle, handle, steeple, dwindle, paddle, bundle, table, castle, waddle, able, cattle, chuckle; 1. Cattle, 2. handle, 3. waddle, 4. dwindle, 5. table, 6. bundle, 7. bottle, 8. castle, 9. chuckle, 10. steeple, 11. able, 12. paddle; 1. Little, people, 2. jungle, example, 3. Bible, Chronicles.

Day 52: Clue: ends, le; Candle, little, spittle, topple, bottle, cuddle, people, trample, puzzle, Bible, tremble, drizzle; 1. Drizzle, 2. spittle, 3. people, 4. candle, 5. Bible, bottle, 6. trample, 7. little, 8. cuddle, 9. tremble, 10. topple, puzzle.

Day 53: Clue: ends, le; (going down) Jingle, trouble, double, tangle, bubble, comfortable, apple, temple, waffle, single, marble, valuable, dimple, scrapple; 1. Temple, 2. apple, 3. scrapple, 4. waffles, 5. double trouble, 6. marble, 7. comfortable, 8. Jingle, 9. single, 10. dimple, 11. bubble, 12. tangle, 13. valuable.

Day 54: Clue: ends, le; (going down) Portable, feeble, pestle, sample, example, circle, cradle, lovable, pimples, tattle, spindle, horrible, rattle, terrible; 1. Spindle, 2. cradle, rattle, 3. terrible, horrible, 4. pimples, 5. example, 6. sample, 7. pestle, 8. portable, 9. lovable, 10. feeble, 11. tattle, 12. circle.

Day 55:   (going across) Ie – A, ie – A, ie – A, ei – B, ie – A, ei – C, ei – B, ei – B, ie – A, ei – C, ie – A, ie – A, ei – C, ie – A, ie – A; 1. Retriever – A, Daniel – A; 2. eight – C, weighs – C; 3. neighbors – C, friend – A; 4. thief – A, piece – A; 5. believe – A, ceiling –B, retrieve – A, weigh – C; 6. tie – A, field – A; 7. deceitful – B.

Day 56: Clue: i, e, c, a, ei, ei, ie; (going across)lie – A, die – A, quiet – A; their – C, conceive – B; chief – A; heir – C, patient – A, friend – A; yield – A, field – A, receive – B; deceived – B, neighbor – C, believe – A; 1. conceive, 2. yield, 3. field, 4. lie, 5. believe, 6. neighbor, 7. heir, 8. patient, 9. receive, 10. deceived, 11. quiet, 12. friend.

Day 57: Clue: i, e, c, a, ei, ei, ie; (going across) pie – A, relieved – A, their – C; audience – A; conceit – B, view – A; mischief – A, fiend – A, review – A; deceit – B, receipt – B, fierce – A; quiet – A, reprieve – A, cashier – A; 1. Review – A, 2. mischief – A, 3. quiet – A, 4. audience – A, 5. fierce – A, 6. their – C, 7. cashier – A receipt – B, 8. relieved – A reprieve – A; 9. pie – A; 10. fiend – A conceited – B, 11. view – A.

Day 58: Clue: i, e, c, a, ei, ei, ie; (going across) friendly – A, reprieve – A, their – C; deceitful – B, patiently – A, quietly – A; heirloom – C, relieved – A, viewing – A; unyielded – A, conceited – B, thieves – A; fiendish – A, audience – A, belief – A; 1. Heirloom – C; 2. relieved – A, fiendish – A, thieves – A; 3. unyielded – A, deceitful – B, conceited – B, belief – A; 4. viewing – A, audience – A; 5. their – C, friendly – A, quietly – A; 6. patiently – A, reprieve – A.

Day 59: Clue: i, e, c, a, ei, ei, ie; (going across) diet – A, experience – A, eighteen – C; eighty – C, briefcase – A, sieve – A; pierce – A, diesel – A, niece – A; siege – A; neighbor – C, their – C; ceiling – B, tiers – A, unwieldy – A; shield – A, pier – A, piety – A; 1. Briefcase – A, eighteen – C; 2. diet – A, eighty – C; 3. pierce – A, shield – A; 4. niece – A, experience – A; 5. their – C, ceiling – B; 6. tiers – A, unwieldy – A, 7. siege – A, piety – A; 8. pier – A, diesel – A; 9. neighbor – C, sieve – A.

Day 60: Clue: -tch,, which, much, such, silent, n, r, lunch, porch; Clue: ends, -le; Clue: i, e, c, a, ei, ei, ie; 1. Piece, candle, patch; 2. Neighbors catch, handle; 3. Fetch, niece's, bottle; 4. Receive batch, people; 5. Uncle, received, watch; 6. Handle, pierced .

Day 61: Creation, Evolution, vacation, notions, station, motion, potion, caption, correction, vaccination; 1. Station, 2. motion, 3. potion, 4. Evolution, 5. creation, 6. caption, 7. vacation, 8. correction, 9. vaccination, 10. notions; 11. Evolutionist, Creationist, 12. correction, caption, 13. vaccination, vacation.

Day 62: Clue: -tion. (going down) Lotion, auction, fiction, action, reaction, commotion, sections, location, dictionary, mention; 1. Lotion, 2. sections, 3. Mention, 4. auction, 5. dictionary, 6. fiction, 7. reaction, 8. action, 9. commotion, 10. location; 11.. Dictionary, reaction, 12. mention, auction.

Day 63: Clue: -tion. 1. Conversation, 2. Salvation, 3. Traditions, 4. Sanctification, 5. Afflictions, 6. Affection, 7. Communication, 8. Creation, 9. Condemnation, 10. Preparation

Day 64: Clue: -tion. 1. Supplication, 2. Temptation, 3. Translation, 4. Tribulations, tribulation, 5. Vexation, 6. Visitation, 7. Vocation, 8. Foundation, 9. Generation, nation.

Day 65: Clue: -tion. (going down) Perfection, completion, damnation, exceptions, fiction, consolation, executions, correction, action, traction; 1. Completion, 2. consolation, 3. fiction, 4. traction, 5. perfection, 6. exceptions, 7. correction, 8. Executions, 9. damnation, 10. action; 11. Perfecshun, consolashun, 12. compleshun, correcshun, 13. tracshun, acshun.

Day 66: 1. Was; 2. Was; 3. Wanted, was; 4. Wanted; 5. What was; 6. Was; 7 What; 8. Wanted; 9. What, was.

Day 67: Clue: was, a, h; Want, h, can't, want; What, what, wh. Across: 1. Was; 3. Want; 4. What; 6. Want; Down: 1. What; 2. Wanted; 4. Want; 5. Was.

Day 68: Clue: was, a, h; Want, h, can't, want; What, what, wh. 1. What, 2. What, 3. What, 4. Wants, 5. Was, 6. Was, was, was, 7. What, what, want, 8. What.

(Page 158)

Day 69: Clue: was, a, h; Want, h, can't, want; What, what, wh. 1. What, what, 2. Wanting, 3. Want, 4. Was, was, 5. Want, 6. Was, 7. What, what, what, what, what, what, what, 8. Wanted.

Day 70: Clue: -tion. Clue: was, a, h; Want, h, can't, want; What, what, wh. Clue: you're, you are, a, you are, you're, your, possession, r; Clue: ends, le; 1. You're, temple; 2. What, education, want; 3. Salvation, was, education; 4. Simple, Bible, handle, situations; 5. Your, additional.

Day 71: Bright, right, light, fight, tight, sight; 1. Bright, 2. tight, 3. sight, 4. light, 5. right, 6. fight; 7. Right, fight, 8. bright, light, 9. sight, tight.

Day 72: Clue: -ight, -gh-; (going down) Blight, fright, might, flight, plight, night; 1. Plight, 2. might, 3. night, 4. blight, 5. flight, 6. fright; 7. Blight, plight, 8. might, flight, 9. fright, nightmare.

Day 73: Clue: -ight, -gh-; 1. Midnight; 2. Right, 3. Lightbulb, 4. Mighty, 5. Bright, 6. Sight, 7. Fight, 8. Tight, 9. Flight, 10. Blighted.

Day 74: Clue: -ight, -gh-; Across: 1. Mighty; 2. Dwight; 5. Lightbulb; 8. Flight; 9. Tight; 10: blight; Down: 1. Midnight; 3. Sight; 4. Plight; 6. Brightly; 7. Right; 8. Fright.

Day 75: 1. Always, 2. Before, 3. Because, 4. Almost, 5. Always, before, 6. Almost, because, 7. Before, because, 8. Almost, always, 9. Always, because.

Day 76: Clue: be, e, because, au, before, for, al, always, ways, almost most. 1. Because, 2. Always before, because, 3. Before, 4. Always, before, 5. Always, 6. Almost, 7. Because, 8. Always, 9. Almost, 10. Before.

Day 77: Clue: be, e, because, au, before, for, al, always, ways, almost most. 1. Because, because, 2. Before, 3. Almost, 4. Because, 5. Almost, 6. Always, 7. Always, 8. Because, 9. Before.

Day 78: Clue: be, e, because, au, before, for, al, always, ways, almost most. 1. Always, 2. Because, 3. Almost, 4. Before, before, 5. Always, because, 6. Before, always, 7. Almost, before, 8. Almost, because.

Day 79: Clue: be, e, because, au, before, for, al, always, ways, almost most. 1. Before, always, 2. Almost, 3. Because, 4. Because, 5. Because, because. 6. Almost, 7. Before, because, 8. Always.

Day 80 Review: Clue: -ight, -gh-; Clue: be, e, because, au, before, for, al, always, ways, almost most. Clue: two, one, missing, doesn't, squeezed, left out, used to be, spell, change, used to be; Clue: -tion. 1. Couldn't, location, because, light; 2. Right, almost, didn't, station; 3. Might, creation, they'd, always, evolution.

Day 81: Across: 3. Marble, 7. Harbor, 9. Park, 10. Alarm, 11. Charter, 14. Garden, 16. Darn, 17. Mars, 18. Market; Down: 1. Far, 2. Smart, 4. Bargain, 5. Car, 6. Darling, 8. Barn, 9. Pardon, 12. Are, 13. Harm, 15. Dark.

Day 82: Clue: -ar, star. 1. Alarm, 2. Arm, 3. Army, 4. Far, 5. Garden, 6. Harm, 7. Harp, 8. Mark, 9. Pardon, 10. Part, part, 11. Sparks, 12. Stars.

Day 83: Clue: -ar, star. 1. Jar, 2. Bars, 3. March, 4. Part, 5. Harp, 6. Shark, 7. Art, 8. Farm, 9. Start, 10. Star, 11. Mark, 12. Smart, 13. Car, 14. Spark, 15. Arms, 16. Dart.

Day 84: Clue: -ar, star. 1. Sharper, 2. Marble, 3. Harmless, 4. Star, 5. Hardness, 6. Market, 7. Marvel, 8. Martyrs, 9. Marred, 10. Harden, 11. Garment, 12. Garlic.

Day 85: (Going down) puncture, legislature, furniture, miniature, literature, rapture, dentures, lecture, featured, adventure; 1. Dentures, 2. Miniature, 3. Literature, 4. Rapture, 5. Lecture, 6. Featured, 7. Puncture, 8. Furniture.

Day 86: Clue: -ture. Across: 1. Literature, 3. Signature, 4. Future, 5. Creature, 6. Furniture, 8. Adventure, 10. Torture, 11. Lecture; Down: 1. Legislature, 2. Rapture, 4. Feature, 6. Fracture, 7. Indenture, 9. Nurture.

Day 87: Clue: -ture. (Going down) tortured, pictures, nature, nurture, Scripture, furniture, pasture, creature, future; 1. Furniture, 2. Pasture, 3. Pictures, 4. Future, 5. Creature, 6. Nurture, 7. Scripture, 8. Tortured, 9. Nature.

Day 88: Clue: -ture. (Going across) tincture, indenture, mature, miniature, featured, literature, fixture, adventures, suture, departure; 1. Adventures, 2. Featured, 3. Fixture, 4. Mature, 5. Suture, tincture, 6. Miniature, 7. Departure.

Day 89: Clue: -ture. Tortured, adventure, mature, legislature, captured, lectured, Scripture, signature, future.

Day 90 Review: Clue: i, e, c, a, ei, ei, ie; Clue: was, a, h; Want, h, can't, want; What, what, wh. Clue: -ar, star. Clue: -ture. 1. What, car; 2. Scriptures, believe, want; 3. Immature, started, furniture, was; 4. Card, piece, natures.

Day 91: 1. Anyone, 2. Already, 3. Sure, 4. Anyone, sure, 5. Already, many, 6. Sure, any, 7. Already, 8. Many 9. Sure, 10. Many, 11. Already, 12. Sure, any, 13. Many, already.

Day 92: Clue: rhyme, a, one, one l, sh, s, su, su, su. 1. Many, 2. Already, 3. Sure, many, 4. Any, 5. Any, 6. Sure, any, 7. Already, 8. Many, any, 9. Already, 10. Sure, 11. Sure, 12. Any, 13. Many.

Day 93: Clue: rhyme, a, one, one l, sh, s, su, su, su. 1. Sure, 2. Already, 3. Any, 4. Many, 5. Already, 6. Already, 7. Many, 8. Any, 9. Many, 10. Sure, 11. Sure, 12. Any.

Day 94: Clue: rhyme, a, one, one l, sh, s, su, su, su. 1. Any, 2. Already, already, 3. Sure, 4. Many, 5. Many, 6. Many, 7. Sure, 8. Already, 9. Any, 10. Already, 11. Sure, 12. Any.

Day 95: (Going down) edge, dredge, hedge, pledge, grudge, fudge, judge, lodge, nudge. 1. Pledge, 2. Judge, 3. Fudge, 4. Nudge, 5. Lodge, 6. Hedge, 7. Dredge, 8. Edge, 9. Grudge.

Day 96: Clue: short, ends, j, dge. 1. Badge, 2. Drudge, 3. Budget, 4. Dredge, 5. Sledge, 6. Midget, 7. Gadget, 8. Grudge, 9. Hodgepodge, 10. Edge, 11. Smudge, 12. Bridge.

Day 97: Clue: short, ends, j, dge. 1. Budge, 2. Wedge, 3. Bridge, 4. Sludge, 5. Pudge, 6. Gadget, 7. Sledge, 8. Badge, 9. Ledge.

Day 98: Clue: short, ends, j, dge. (Going down) badger, hedge, pledge, edge, judge, lodge, grudge, ledges, wedge. 1. Judge, judge; 2. Edge; 3. Grudge, 4. Hedge, 5. Lodge, lodge, 6. Pledge, 7. Badger, 8. Ledges, ledges, 9. Wedge.

Day 99: Clue: short, ends, j, dge. 1. Nudge, edge, 2. Lodge, hodgepodge, 3. Judge, grudge, 4. Midget, budget, 5. Dredge, bridge, 6. Fudge, wedge, 7. Hedge, gadget, 8. Budge, badge, 9. Sludge, smudge.

Day 100 Review: Clue: -ight, -gh-; Clue: be, e, because, au, before, for, al, always, ways, almost most. Clue: rhyme, a, one, one l, sh, s, su, su, su. Clue: -Dge. 1. Many, light, because; 2. Almost, always, before, any; 3. Sure, already, before, bright; 4. Fight, edged, hedged.

Day 101: 1. Cord, 2. Sports, 3. Ford, 4. Storms, 5. Thorns, 6. Short, 7. Lord, 8. Pork, 9. Stork, 10. Porch, 11. Horse, 12. Torn.

Day 102: Clue: -or, consonant, -ore, -r, four. Across: 3. Ore, 4. Fork, 6. Morning, 7. Stories, 9. Thorn, 11. Dories, 13. Jordan, 14. Horse; Down: 1. Horn, 2. Torn, 4. Force, 5. Vortex, 7. Scorn, 8. Sports, 10. North, 12. Short.

(Page 160)

Day 103: Clue: -or, consonant, -ore, -r, four. 1. Shore, 2. Core, 3. Sore, 4. Or, nor, 5. Report, 6. Record, 7. Platform, 8. Lord, 9. More, 10. Story, 11. Forms, 12. North, 13. Cord.

Day 104: Clue: -or, consonant, -ore, -r, four. 1. Lord, horse, 2. Lord, glory, 3. Lord, before, Jordan, 4. Morning, Lord, morning, 5. For, sword, 6. Storm, 7. Stork, 8. Thorns, 9. Exhort, 10. Conformed, transformed, 11. Born.

Day 105: 1. Do do, 2. Only, 3. Of, 4. Who, 5. Only of, 6. Who, do, 7. Of, 8. Of, 9. Who, 10. Only, 11. Do, of, 12. Only, do, 13. Who, of, 14. Only, 15. Who.

Day 106: Clue: o, do, done, w, two, of, o, f, o. 1. Who, 2. Who, 3. Who, of, 4. Who, of, of, do, of, 5. Do, 6. Who, of, 7. Who, only, doing, do, do, 8. Do, doing, who, done, 9. Done.

Day 107: Clue: o, do, done, w, two, of, o, f, o. 1. Only, 2. Of, 3. Do, do, 4. Who, of, only who, of, who, 5. Who, of, who, 6. Who, of, who, 7. Who, of, 8. Of, 9. Do, of.

Day 108: Clue: o, do, done, w, two, of, o, f, o.1. of, do, 2. Of, do, 3. Who only, 4. Who, 5. Only, do, 6. Do, who, 7. Only, who, of, 8. Of, only, 9. Only, of, 10. Do, of, 11. Do, do, 12. Of, only.

Day 109: Clue: o, do, done, w, two, of, o, f, o. 1. Who, only, 2. Of, of, who, 3. Only, 4. Who, 5. Who, who, 6. Do, 7. Of, 8. Of, 9. Do, of, 10. Who, who, of.

Day 110: Clue: -or, consonant, -ore, -r, four. : Clue: o, do, done, w, two, of, o, f, o. Clue: -ar, star. Clue: -ture. 1. Of, pictures, do, farmer's, market, 2. Only, who, of, storm, 3. Do, force, capture, 4. Morning, who, of, Jordan, who, garden of.

Day 111: 1. Late, 2. Ace, 3. Grace, 4. Sale, 5. Grape, 6. Made, 7. Grade, 8. Ate, 9. Bake, cake, 10. Names, games.

Day 112: Clue: ai, a, e, ay. 1. Flame, 2. Planes, 3. Share, 4. Base, 5. Safe, 6. Save, 7. Hate, 8. Page, 9. Place, 10. Stage, 11. Males, females.

Day 113: Clue: ai, a, e, ay. 1. Paid, 2. Bail, 3. Raid, 4. Failed, 5. Hail, 6. Sail, 7. Mail, 8. Chair, 9. Pair, 10. hair, 11. Nail, 12. Plain.

Day 114: Clue: ai, a, e, ay. 1. Claim, 2. Trail, 3. Jail, 4. Snail, 5. Air, 6. Gain, 7. Main, 8. Rain, 9. Brain, 10. Spain, 11. Pain, 12. Train.

Day 115: Clue: ai, a, e, ay. 1. Day, 2. Pay, 3. Gray, 4. Jay, 5. Stray, 6. Ray, 7. Holidays, 8. Say, 9. Play, 10. Stay, 11. Bay, 12. Way.

Day 116: Clue: ai, a, e, ay. 1. Fray, 2. Kay, 3. Gay, 4. Slay, 5. May, 6. Hay, 7. Clay, 8. Pray, 9. Tray, 10. Sway, 11. Cray, 12. Dismay.

Day 117: Clue: ai, a, e, ay. 1. Blue jay, 2. Crate, 3. Holidays, 4. Lakes, 5. Pray, 6. Remains, 7. Saint, 8. Scales, 9. Slate, 10. Stain, 11. Tame, 12. Train, 13. Brain.

Day 118: Clue: ai, a, e, ay.1. rain, 2. Gates, 3. Faint, 4. Lame, 5. Disgrace, name, 6. Shake, place, 7. Behave, 8. Face, face, 9. Pray, 10. Faith.

Day 119: Clue: ai, a, e, ay. Across: 5. Fairy tale, 7. Lane, 9. Prepay, 10. Mistake, 11. Scrape, 13. Snare, 14. Parade, 15. Shave. Down: 1. Spray, 2. Stale, 3. Plate, 4. Snakes, 6. Lemonade, 8. Sprain, 11. Scare, 12. Drape.

Day 120 Review: Clue: ai, a, e, ay. Clue: i, e, c, a, ei, ei, ie; Clue: rhyme, a, one, one l, sh, s, su, su, su. Clue: -dge. 1. Belief, judge, fail, many; 2. Any, saved, grace, faith; 3. Fields, already, many, edge, gates; 4. Pray, rain, faint, face, face.

Day 121: 1. Cone, 2. Expose, 3. Prone, 4. Rose, 5. Chose, 6. Code, 7. Vote, 8. Rope, 9. Slope, 10. Hose, 11. Drove, 12. Drone.

Day 122: Clue: o, e, oa, ow, o, oe. 1. Bones, 2. Nose, 3. Phone, 4. Hope, 5. Scope, 6. Dope, 7. Pope, 8. Close, 9. Tote, 10. Coke, 11. Pose, 12. Dove.

Day 123: Clue: o, e, oa, ow, o, oe. 1. Coax, 2. Boat, 3. Soap, 4. Coal, 5. Loan, 6. Load, 7. Road, 8. Toad, 9. Soak, 10. Groan, 11. Bloat, 12. Cloak.

Day 124: Clue: o, e, oa, ow, o, oe. 1. Toast, 2. Throat, 3. Coat, 4. Oats, 5. Croak, 6. Foal, 7. Moan, 8. Goal, 9. Boast, 10. Moat, 11. Coast, 12. Roast.

Day 125: Clue: o, e, oa, ow, o, oe. 1. Blow, 2. Toes, 3. Go, 4. Row, 5. Snow, 6. Grow, 7. Woe, 8. Crow, 9. No, 10. Slow, 11. Foe, 12. Throw.

Day 126: Clue: o, e, oa, ow, o, oe. 1. Glow, 2. Know, 3. Show, 4. Flow, 5. So, 6. Bow, 7. Sow, 8. Low, 9. Mow, 10. Joe, 11. Hoe, 12. Tow.

Day 127: Clue: o, e, oa, ow, o, oe. 1. Rome, 2. Hole, 3. Robe, 4. Smoke, 5. Strove, 6. Goats, 7. Loaf, boat, 8. Oak, 9. Suppose.

Day 128: Clue: o, e, oa, ow, o, oe. 1. Joke, 2. Float, 3. Yoyo, 4. Mole, 5. Gloat, 6. Grove, 7. Quo, 8. Joan, 9. Zone, 10. Froze, 11. Foam, 12. Roam, 13. Oath.

Day 129: Clue: o, e, oa, ow, o, oe. Across: 2. Photo, 3. Clove, 4. Note, 6. Remote, 7. Piano, 8. Woke, 9. Quote, 10. Potato. Down: 1. Stove, 3. Choke, 5. Home, 6. Rowboat.

Day 130 Review: Clue: o, e, oa, ow, o, oe. Clue: two, one, missing, doesn't, squeezed, left out, used to be, spell, change, used to be; Clue: y, y, i, suffix, not, y, i, vowels, not, y, i, i, row; Clue: ends, -le. 1. There's, home, happiest, memories, table; 2. Isn't families, supposed, examples, we're, He's. 3. Able, those, families, aren't, able, able.

Day 131: 1. Are, 2. Said, again, 3. Again, 4. Are, 5. Are, 6. Said, 7. Said, 8. Again, 9. Are, 10. Said, 11. Again, 12. Are, 13. Said.

Day 132: Clue: said, sa, e, a. 1. Again, said, 2. Are, 3. Again, 4. Are, are, 5. Are, 6. Said, 7. Again, 8. Said, 9. Are.

Day 133: Clue: said, sa, e, a. 1. Again, 2. Said, 3. Again, 4. Are, 5. Are, 6. Said, 7. Are, 8. Again, 9. Said.

Day 134: Clue: said, sa, e, a. 1. Said, 2. Again, 3. Are, 4. Said, 5. Said, 6. Again, 7. Again, 8. Are, 9. Are, 10. Said, 11. Are, 12. Are, again.

Day 135: Clue: said, sa, e, a. 1. Again, 2. Are, 3. Are, 4. Said, 5. Again, 6. Said, 7. Are, 8. Said, 9. Again, 10. Are, 11. Again, 12. Said.

Day 136: 1. Does, 2. Have, 3. Can, 4. From, 5. Does, 6. From, 7. Can, 8. Have, 9. Does, 10. From.

Day 137: Clue: does, es, o, o, from, to, a, a, ave, ave, can, can't, can. 1. Can, 2. Does, from, from, 3. Have, 4. Have, 5. From, 6. Does, 7. Can, from, can, from, 8. From.

(Page 162)

Day 138: Clue: does, es, o, o, from, to, a, a, ave, ave, can, can't, can. 1. Does, have, can, 2. From, 3. From, can, 4. Does, from, 5. Can, 6. Can, have, 7. Does, have, 8. Does, have, from, 9. Can, from.

Day 139: Clue: does, es, o, o, from, to, a, a, ave, ave, can, can't, can. 1. From, 2. Have, have, 3. From, have, 4. Can, 5. Does, 6. Can, can, 7. From, from, 8. Does, does, does.

Day 140: Clue: does, es, o, o, from, to, a, a, ave, ave, can, can't, can. Clue: said, sa, e, a. Clue: be, e, because, au, before, for, al, always, ways, almost most. Clue: -dge. 1. Are, fudge, because, can, almost, before, does. 2. Always, edge, again, does, from, edge. 3. Can, have, badge.

Day 141: 1. Mean, 2. Seat, 3. Heat, 4. Fear, 5. Beans, 6. Clean, 7. Teach, 8. Wheat, 9. Team, 10. Year, 11. Meal, 12. Bleach.

Day 142: Clue: ea, ee. 1. Seek, 2. Trees, 3. Greedy, 4. Need, 5. Sleep, 6. Keep, 7. Feed, sheep, 8. Weep, 9. Feet, 10. Sweet, 11. Meek.

Day 143: Clue: ea, ee. 1. Heel, heal, 2. Dear, deer, 3. Week, weak, 4. Beet, beat, 5. Read, reed, 6. Team, teem, 7. Flea, flee, 8. See, sea, 9. Meet, meat, 10. Peek, peak, 11. Seem, seam.

Day 144: Clue: ea, ee. 1. bees, 2. Free, 3. Cheer, 4. Creep, 5. Weeds, 6. Street, 7. Beef, 8. Feel, 9. Three, 10. Knee, 11. Queen, 12. Screen.

Day 145: Clue: ea, ee. 1. Weak, 2. Reap, 3. Hear, hear, 4. Each, 5. Preach, 6. Feast, 7. Leap, 8. Clean, 9. Heal, 10. Fear, fear, 1. Near, near.

Day 146: Clue: ea, ee. Across: 3. Treat, 4. Gear, 6. Year, 7. Cream, 9. Lean, 11. Cheek, 12. East, 14. Heat, 15. Clean. Down: 1. Stream, 2. Streak, 5. Real, 7. Creed, 8. Wheel, 10. Neat, 13. Seed.

Day 147: Clue: ea, ee. 1. Steam, 2. Steer, 3. Teen, 4. Sheets, 5. Greet, 6. Sweep, 7. Green, 8. Veal, 9. Tea, 10. Leaf, 11. Beads, 12. Peach.

Day 148: Clue: ea, ee. 1. Beast, 2. Three, 3. Yeast, 4. Beef, 5. Zeal, 6. Steep, 7. Mean, 8. Deep, 9. Speak, 10. Queen bee, 11. Read.

Day 149: Clue: ea, ee. 1. Breed, 2. Fear, 3. Dream, 4. Weep, 5. Deer, 6. Speed, 7. Week, 8. Peas, 9. Tear, 10. Beak, 11. Seal, 12. Cheat.

Day 150: Clue: ea, ee. Clue: o, e, oa, ow, o, oe. Clue: ai, a, e, ay. Clue: does, es, o, o, from, to, a, a, ave, ave, can, can't, can. 1. Came, home, train, from, east, coast. 2. Does, have, from, teacher, week's. 3. Hope, faith, saves, from, said, clean, grace.

Congratulations! You did it!

Ordering Information

Schoolhouse Publishing has many unique and wonderful books that will build your student's faith and enhance your student's academic progress. We also provide books for homeschool moms, to encourage your heart and make your homeschool endeavor easier. Our books are easy to use, enjoyable, require no teacher preparation, and are widely acclaimed. Below is a sampling of our most popular books:

- *Apples Daily Spelling Drills for Secondary Students*
- *Apples 2 Daily Phonics Drills for Secondary Students*
- *Fencing Lessons (Bible study for middle schoolers)*
- *Homeschool Supermom…NOT!*
- *Come to the Garden (study guide for Homeschool Supermom…NOT!)*
- *Pennsylvania Keystones (PA History for elementary students)*
- *Research in Increments (writing a research paper…made easy)*
- *Word Artist (a study of poetry for all ages)*
- *Caution: for Boys (fun creative writing ideas for young writers)*
- *Caution: for Girls (fun creative writing ideas for young writers)*
- *The Log (a simple record-keeping system for your homeschool)*

For more information, visit our website:

www.shpublishing.com